YE OLDE

NATIONAL GEOGRAPHIC KiDS

weird but true!

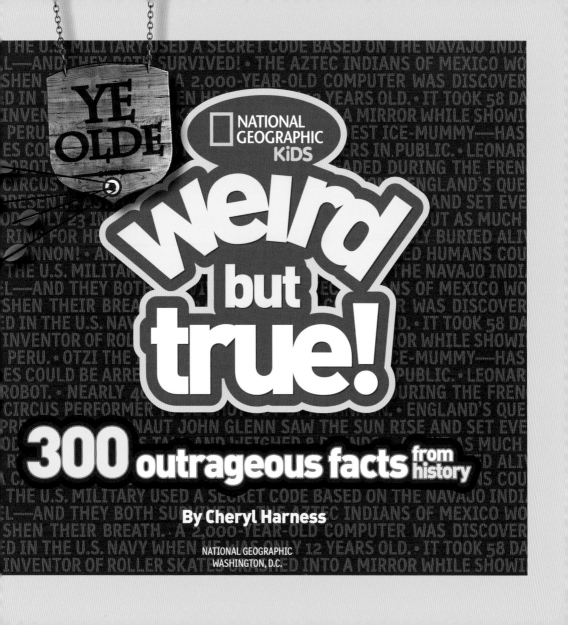

YE OLDE

NATIONAL GEOGRAPHIC KiDS

weird but true!

300 outrageous facts from history

By Cheryl Harness

NATIONAL GEOGRAPHIC
WASHINGTON, D.C.

Visit us online:
Kids: natgeokids.com
Parents: nationalgeographic.com/books
Librarians and teachers: nationalgeographic
.com/books/librarians-and-educators

For rights or permissions inquiries,
please contact National Geographic Books
Subsidiary Rights: bookrights@natgeo.com

ISBN (Trade): 978-1-4263-1382-0
ISBN (Library): 978-1-4263-1383-7

Printed in China
21/PPS/6 (SC)
21/PPS/4 (RLB)

TOMATOES WERE CONSIDERED POISONOUS UNTIL THE 1800s.

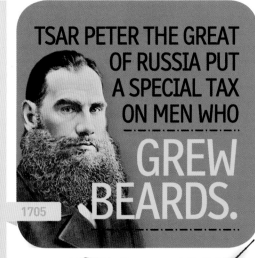

A.D. 1200–1532

The Inca of South America built more than **20,000 MILES OF ROADS,** but had no wheels or horses to ride on them.

THAT'S WEIRD!

TSAR PETER THE GREAT OF RUSSIA PUT A SPECIAL TAX ON MEN WHO **GREW BEARDS.**

1705

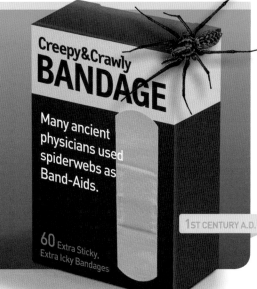

Creepy&Crawly **BANDAGE**

Many ancient physicians used spiderwebs as Band-Aids.

60 Extra Sticky, Extra Icky Bandages

1ST CENTURY A.D.

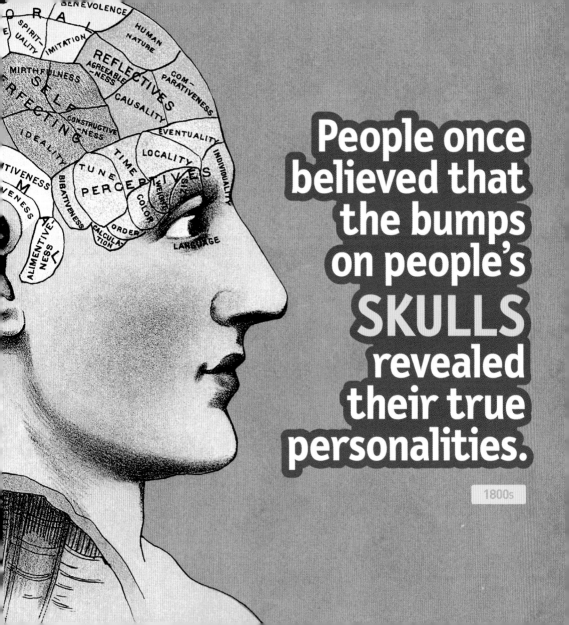

People once believed that the bumps on people's **SKULLS** revealed their true personalities.

1800s

THERE WERE NO DINNER PLATES IN MEDIEVAL TIMES. DINNER WAS SERVED UPON SLABS OF STALE BREAD.

A.D. 500–1000

1815

The War of 1812's last battle was fought two weeks after a peace treaty was signed.

A.D. 1000–PRESENT

An ancient Chinese soup recipe contains simmered BIRDS' NESTS.

MEDIEVAL JAPANESE WOMEN GREW THEIR HAIR AS LONG AS 23 FEET (7M)!

A.D. 794–1185

Some **three million** sunken ships lie on the ocean floor.

10

French queen **MARIE DE MÉDICIS** had 30,000 pearls and

Kids in southern Asia **PLAYED WITH ACTION TOYS** more than 4,400 years ago.

England's Queen Elizabeth I's

TEETH TURNED BLACK

in her old age.

a gown that glittered with more than

3,000

diamonds.

Medieval doctors wore **BIRD MASKS STUFFED WITH HERBS** to ward off bad smells.

A.D. 500–1500

13

Creative American pioneers attached sails to their wagons, zooming up to 40 MILES (64 km) **AN HOUR.**

1860s

EGYPT'S GREAT PYRAMID OF GIZA IS THE ONLY **ANCIENT WONDER OF THE WORLD** THAT IS STILL STANDING.

Queen Elizabeth I whitened her face with white lead and vinegar.

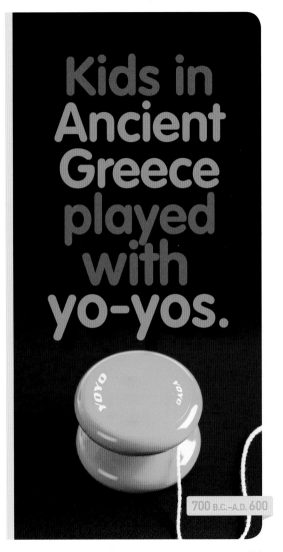

Kids in Ancient Greece played with yo-yos.

700 B.C.–A.D. 600

17

EUROPEAN PREHISTORIC HEALERS

DRILLED HOLES

IN THEIR PATIENTS' SKULLS TO LET THE EVIL SPIRITS OUT.

8000 B.C.

ALEXANDER THE GREAT'S COFFIN WAS FILLED WITH BEESWAX AND HONEY TO PRESERVE HIS BODY.

323 B.C.

In the Middle Ages, ordinary people's birthday celebrations fell on the closest holiday to the day they were born. A.D. 500–1500

Victorian parents used their children's birthday parties to teach them manners. 1800s

For almost 100 years, the monarchs of Great Britain have sent birthday cards to British citizens turning 100 and 105 years old.

Only royalty celebrated birthdays in ancient Egypt. 3000–342 B.C.

In ancient Rome, the traditional birthday food was porridge!
800 B.C.–A.D. 476

Throwing birthday parties for kids didn't become popular until the early 19th century in Germany.

The oldest woman ever, Jeanne Calment, had 122 birthdays!
1875–1997

Greeks started the tradition of lighting candles on birthdays.
700 B.C.–A.D. 600

In some Asian cultures, a person's 61st birthday was traditionally considered their only true birthday—people believed this was the beginning of a new life cycle.

It's traditional in China for birthday boys and girls to slurp up a bowl of long noodles.

The melody of "Happy Birthday to You" was written by two sisters from Kentucky, U.S.A.
1893

21

IN THE MIDDLE AGES,

ONLY RICH PEOPLE

ATE WHITE BREAD.

An inventor once designed **DIAPERS FOR BIRDS.** 1956

George Washington was once an officer in the British Army HE ENDED UP DEFEATING in the American Revolution. 1752–1758

23

GROUND-UP EGYPTIAN MUMMIES

were used to make brown paint.

ANCIENT UMBER
MUMMY'S FINEST

A traditional Korean tonic
was made from

RICE WINE
AND
BABY MICE.

26

Play-Doh was originally used to remove stains from walls.

1956

A U.S. Civil War soldier **COUGHED UP A BULLET** nearly 60 years after he was shot.

1921

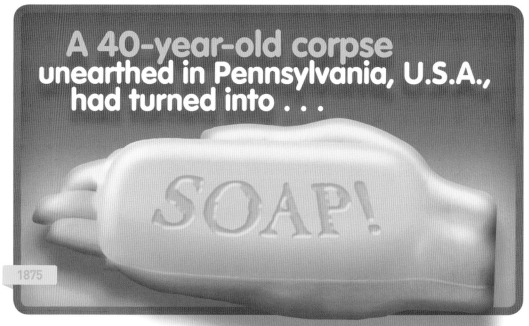

A 40-year-old corpse unearthed in Pennsylvania, U.S.A., had turned into . . . SOAP!

1875

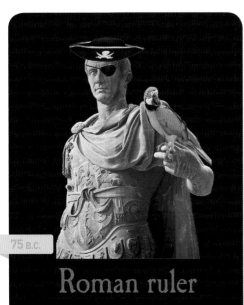

Roman ruler
JULIUS CAESAR
was once
captured by
PIRATES.

TO AVOID BEING BURIED ALIVE, FAIRY TALE AUTHOR HANS CHRISTIAN ANDERSEN KEPT A NOTE BY HIS BED THAT SAID:

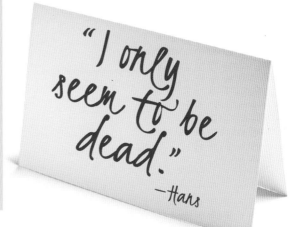

"I only seem to be dead."
—Hans

George Washington's dentures were made from hippopotamus ivory.

1780s

Military salutes
started with
medieval knights, who

RAISED THEIR
VISORS

to reveal their identities
to superiors.

1861–1865

DURING THE U.S. CIVIL WAR, **AMPUTATION SURGERY** TOOK AN AVERAGE OF **THREE MINUTES.**

A MEDIEVAL JAPANESE EMPEROR

OUTLAWED

EATING MEAT.

A.D. 675

A schoolteacher of **THOMAS EDISON,** inventor of the lightbulb, thought he was too "addle-brained" to ever learn anything.

1841

1855

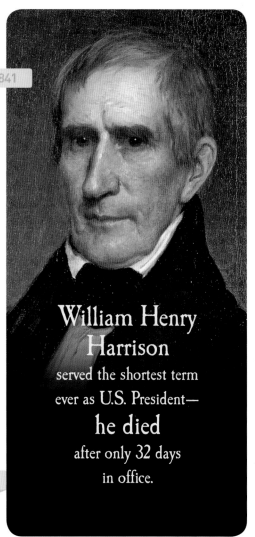

William Henry Harrison served the shortest term ever as U.S. President— **he died** after only 32 days in office.

35

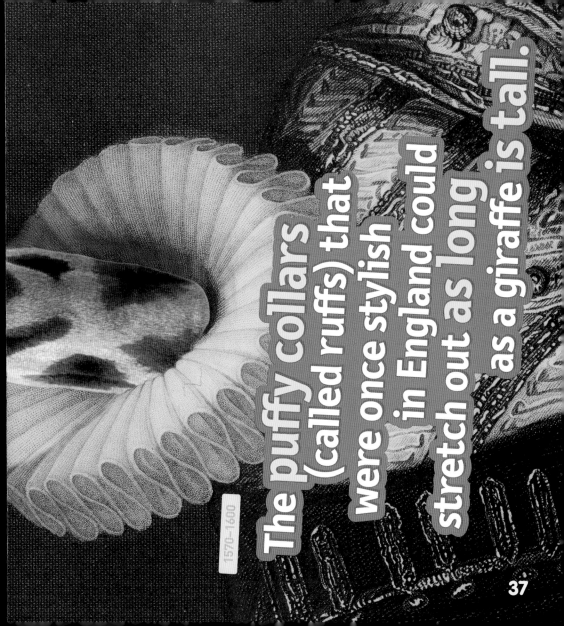

The puffy collars (called ruffs) that were once stylish in England could stretch out as long as a giraffe is tall.

1570–1600

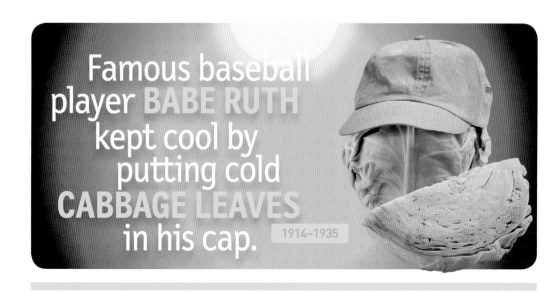

Famous baseball player **BABE RUTH** kept cool by putting cold **CABBAGE LEAVES** in his cap.

1914–1935

THE OLDEST KNOWN MUSICAL INSTRUMENT

is a 42,000-year-old flute made out of a vulture bone.

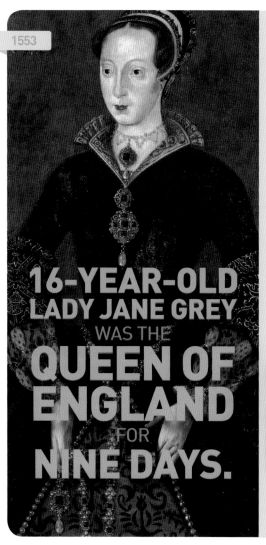

1553

16-YEAR-OLD LADY JANE GREY WAS THE **QUEEN OF ENGLAND** FOR **NINE DAYS.**

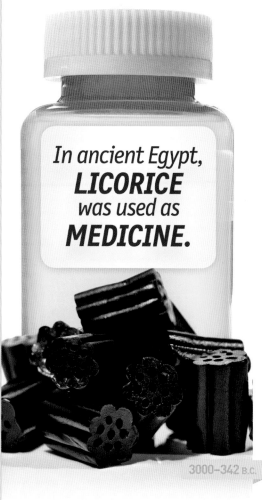

In ancient Egypt, **LICORICE** *was used as* **MEDICINE.**

3000–342 B.C.

39

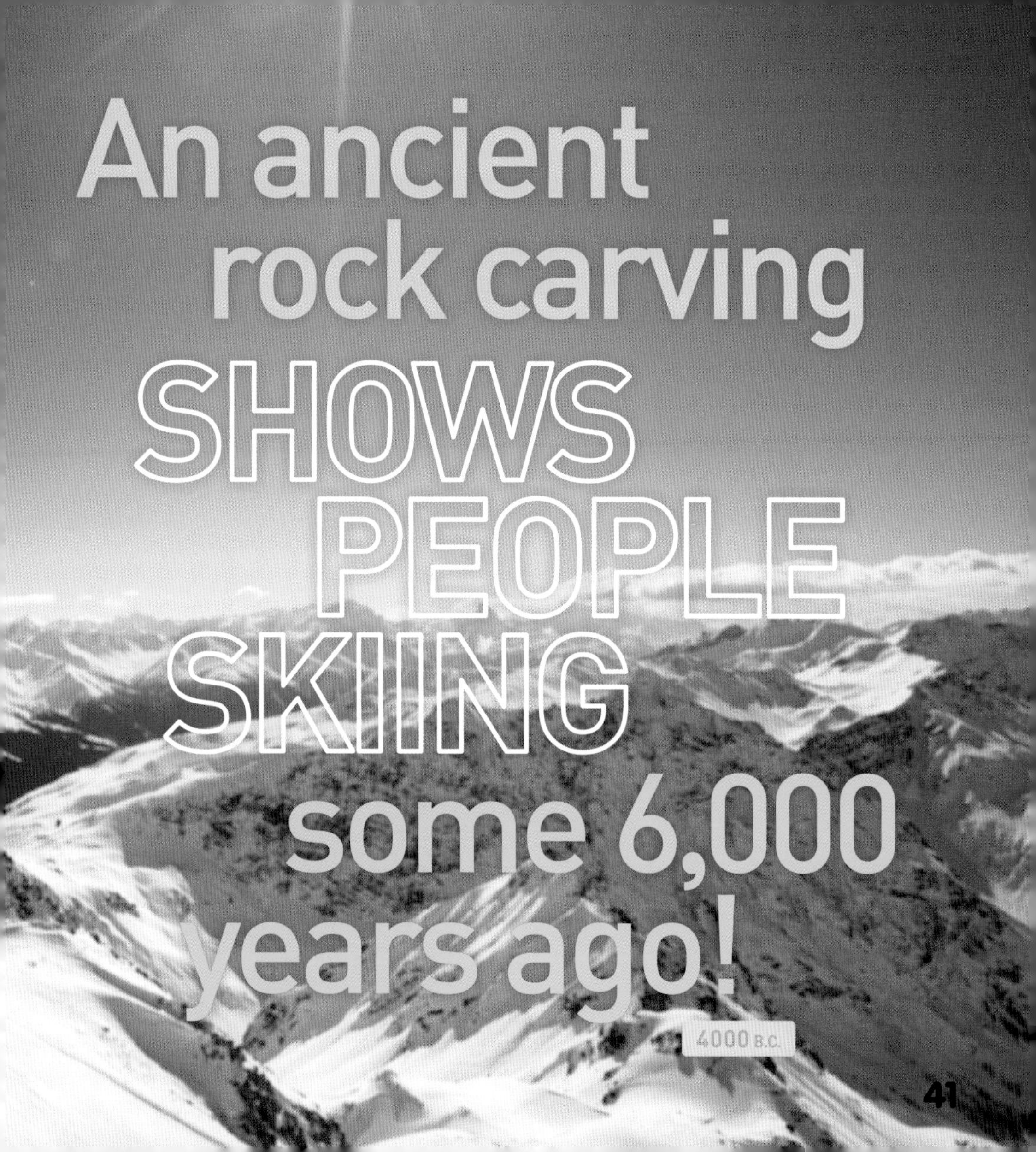

An ancient
rock carving
SHOWS
PEOPLE
SKIING
some 6,000
years ago!

4000 B.C.

The Aztec of ancient Mexico used **COCOA BEANS** as money.

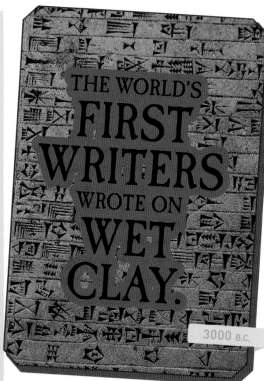

THE WORLD'S **FIRST WRITERS** WROTE ON **WET CLAY.**

3000 B.C.

THAT'S WEIRD!

AT AN ANCIENT ROMAN FEAST, DINERS WERE SERVED A **CHICKEN** STUFFED INSIDE A **DUCK,** INSIDE A **GOOSE,** INSIDE A **PIG,** INSIDE A **COW.**

GROVER CLEVELAND WAS THE ONLY U.S. PRESIDENT TO GET MARRIED IN THE WHITE HOUSE.

In ancient China, some kites **were big enough for people to ride on.**

500 A.D.

800 B.C. – A.D. 476

43

Trains once had cow catchers on the front to knock

stray cattle off the tracks.

1838

1850

More than 140 years after he died, former U.S. President Zachary Taylor's body was dug up to see if he'd been POISONED.

(He hadn't.)

Sailors from the Middle East used to make purple dye from **sea snail mucus.**

1100 B.C.–850 B.C.

One inventor designed

**safety
glasses
for
chickens**

to keep the poultry
from pecking each other.

45

Persian toothpaste was made out of crushed ashes, cattle hooves, eggshells, and oyster shells.

A.D. 1000

700 B.C.–A.D. 600

THROUGHOUT THE ANCIENT WORLD, **mustard** WAS USED AS A MEDICINE FOR EVERYTHING FROM SNAKEBITES TO CONGESTION.

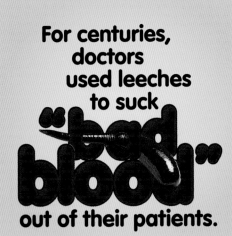

For centuries, doctors used leeches to suck **"bad" blood** out of their patients.

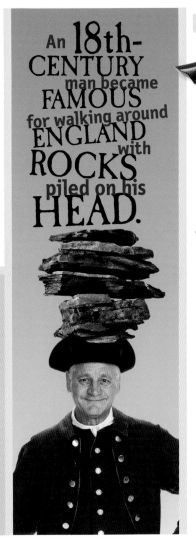

An **18th-CENTURY** man became **FAMOUS** for walking around **ENGLAND** with **ROCKS** piled on his **HEAD.**

1860s–1870s

When popular British princess Alexandra had a stiff leg, it became trendy for Londoners to LIMP ON PURPOSE.

1891

An American man left money so servants could care for his house for 59 years after his death—

in case he was reincarnated!

For centuries,
European women used
**POISONOUS
LEAD**
in their
MAKEUP.

STARTING IN 1500

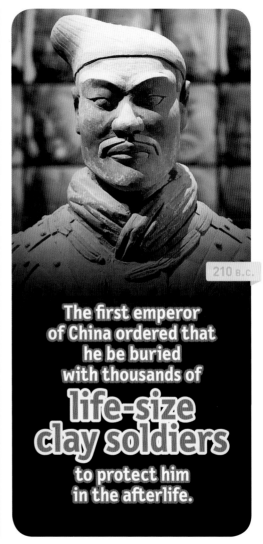

210 B.C.

The first emperor
of China ordered that
he be buried
with thousands of
**life-size
clay soldiers**
to protect him
in the afterlife.

49

Mary Queen of Scots WAS BEHEADED, but her little dog survived by hiding **UNDER HER DRESS.**

1587

In ancient Rome, slaves plucked out unsightly

body hair

from rich people's skin.

800 B.C.–A.D. 476

The shoes of fashionable Italians were once so

1500s

TALL

they had to walk with servants to keep from falling over.

Ancient Greeks and Romans often ate **salted fish that had rotted in the sun** for at least a month.

ca 1200 B.C.

No one knows why the ancient Olmec of Mexico carved

GIANT
STONE HEADS
that weigh as much as
50 TONS!
(45 t)

51

Deimos

Phobos

52

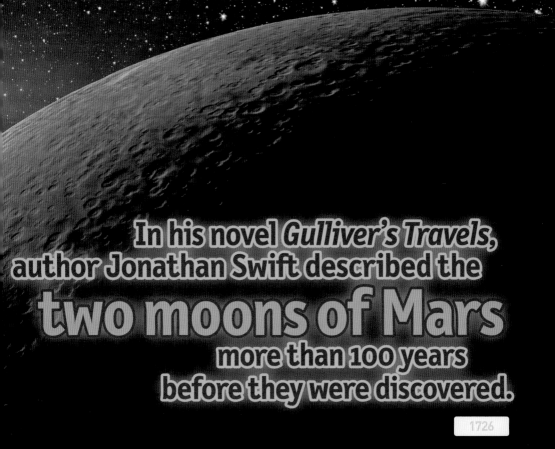

In his novel *Gulliver's Travels*, author Jonathan Swift described the **two moons of Mars** more than 100 years before they were discovered.

1726

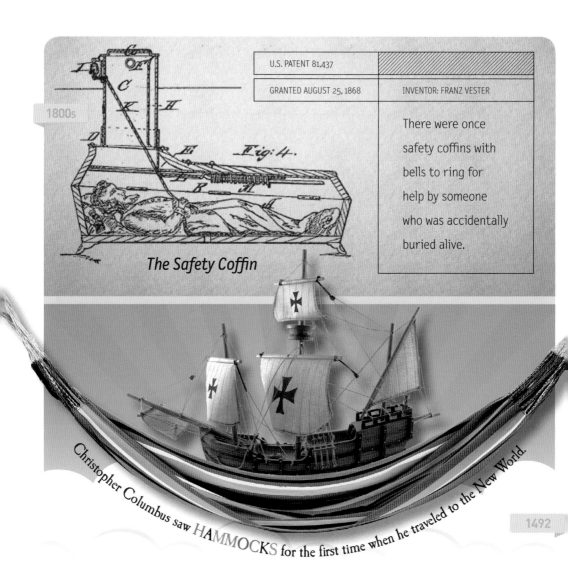

U.S. PATENT 81,437

GRANTED AUGUST 25, 1868   INVENTOR: FRANZ VESTER

There were once safety coffins with bells to ring for help by someone who was accidentally buried alive.

Fig. 4.

The Safety Coffin

1800s

Christopher Columbus saw HAMMOCKS for the first time when he traveled to the New World.

1492

54

1901

A woman and her kitten went over **Niagara Falls** in a barrel— and they both survived!

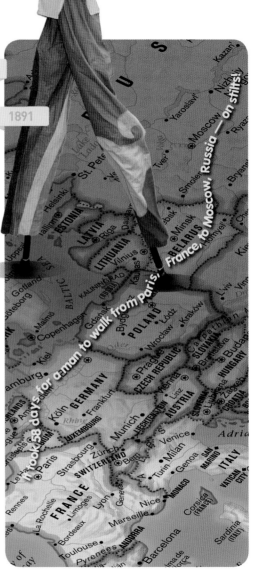

1891

It took 58 days for a man to walk from Paris, France, to Moscow, Russia — on stilts!

A 2,000-year-old "COMPUTER" was discovered inside an ANCIENT GREEK SHIPWRECK.

1901

1760

The man credited with inventing **roller skates crashed** into a mirror while showing off his new invention.

ANCIENT GREEK THINKER PLATO BELIEVED HUMANS COULD SEE BECAUSE **LIGHT RAYS** SHOT OUT OF THEIR **EYEBALLS**

427–347 B.C.

57

Fashionable English ladies used to wear fake eyebrows made of

mouse skin.

England's Queen Victoria received a **1,000-pound (454-kg) wheel of cheddar cheese** as a wedding present.

1840

1800s

19TH-CENTURY DOCTORS SOMETIMES

CLEANED

WOUNDS WITH

MAGGOTS.

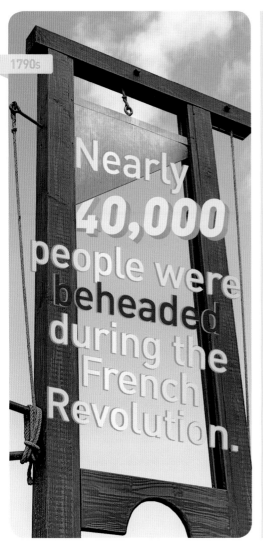

1790s

Nearly **40,000** people were beheaded during the French Revolution.

LIVED 1452–1506

Leonardo da Vinci, who painted the "Mona Lisa," also designed the first humanlike robot.

After a tank burst, an of sticky molasses of Boston,

8-foot (2.4-m) wave flooded the streets Massachusetts, U.S.A.

IN THE 1800s, WOMEN IN THE UNITED STATES COULD BE ARRESTED FOR WEARING TROUSERS IN PUBLIC.

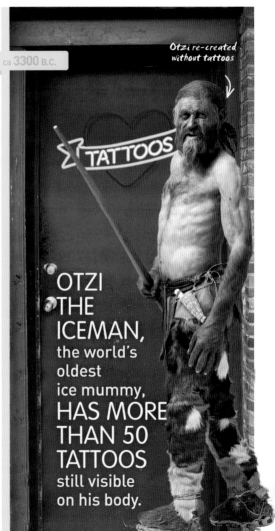

ca 3300 B.C.

Otzi re-created without tattoos

TATTOOS

OTZI THE ICEMAN, the world's oldest ice mummy, **HAS MORE THAN 50 TATTOOS** still visible on his body.

Astronaut John Glenn saw the sun rise and set every 45 minutes during his three orbits of Earth.

1962

1841

SAILORS IN SOUTH AMERICA WON A NAVAL BATTLE BY **FIRING CHEESE** OUT OF A CANNON!

~~████~~ during ████

Navajo Indian

~~████~~ developed an

(secret) code ~~████~~

native language

the U.S. military.

World War II, soldiers ▮▮▮▮▮ unbreakable ▮▮▮▮▮ based on their for ▮▮▮▮▮

A boy lied about his age and enlisted in the **U.S. NAVY** when he was only **12 YEARS OLD.**

1942

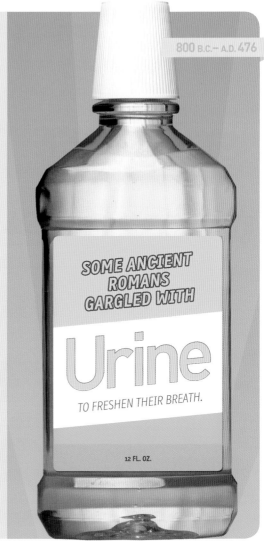

800 B.C.– A.D. 476

SOME ANCIENT ROMANS GARGLED WITH

Urine

TO FRESHEN THEIR BREATH.

12 FL. OZ.

The Aztec of Mexico wore popcorn as jewelry.

EARLY 1500s

1877

Fourteen-year-old Rosa "Zazel" Richter of England was the first circus performer to be **SHOT OUT OF A CANNON.**

GEO. WEBB LITH LONDON.

69

TO HELP
PEOPLE
ESCAPE
FROM
BURNING
BUILDINGS,
A MAN
DEVISED
A PERSONAL

FIRE ESCAPE SUIT WITH A HAT-PARACHUTE.

The shortest woman on record stood only **23 inches** (58 cm) tall— as long as the average house cat.

1876–1895

1940s–1970s

It was once **ILLEGAL** to play pinball in New York City. U.S.A.

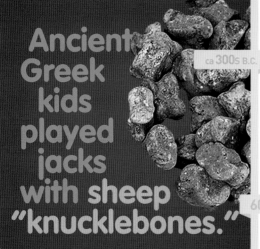

Ancient Greek kids played jacks with sheep "knucklebones."

ca 300s B.C.

TO LOOK FIERCE, SOME

maya filed their teeth

600 B.C.–A.D. 700

INTO SHARP POINTS.

AS MANY
AS 1,600
ANCIENT
ROMANS

TOOK BATHS
TOGETHER
AT THE
SAME TIME.

3RD CENTURY A.D.

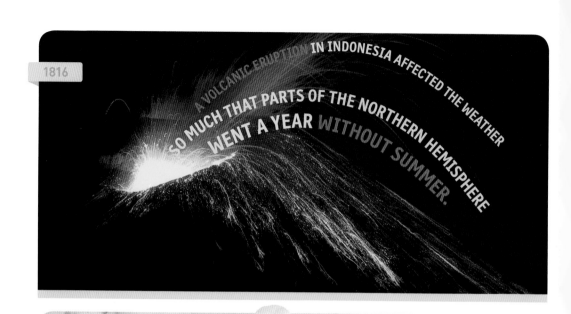

1816 A VOLCANIC ERUPTION IN INDONESIA AFFECTED THE WEATHER SO MUCH THAT PARTS OF THE NORTHERN HEMISPHERE WENT A YEAR WITHOUT SUMMER.

During the **U.S. Civil War,** some **10,000 Confederate** soldiers had one of the **biggest snowball fights** in history.

1863

SUSPECTED VAMPIRES

were sometimes buried with bricks over their mouths.

INMATE   #1003-432

A pig was once
tried for murder.

1494

N

ENGLISH AUTHOR
Charles Dickens

S

CARRIED A COMPASS SO HE COULD
ALWAYS SLEEP FACING NORTH.

1800s

THE GAME
CHINESE
CHECKERS
WAS INVENTED IN
GERMANY.

1892

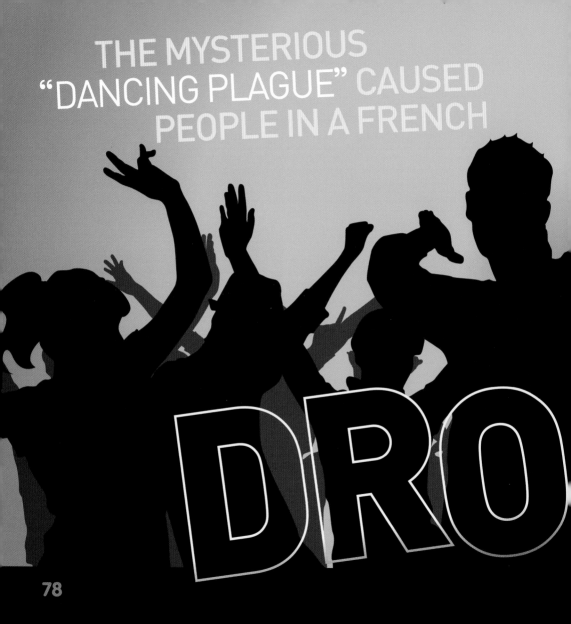

THE MYSTERIOUS
"DANCING PLAGUE" CAUSED
PEOPLE IN A FRENCH

DRO

TOWN TO LITERALLY 1518

DANCE UNTIL THEY

PPED!

MANY ANCIENT ROMAN STATUES HAD INTERCHANGEABLE HEADS THAT COULD BE SWITCHED TO LOOK LIKE THE MOST **RECENT LEADER.**

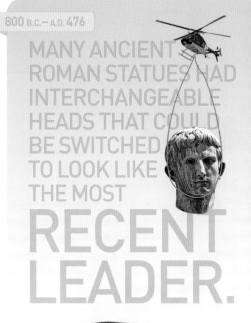

1960

The inventor of the trampoline showed off his creation by jumping on it with a **live kangaroo.**

80

Londoners once believed that **COFFEE** could cure sore eyes.

1650

When **BANANAS** were first sold in the United States, the rare fruit cost the equivalent of

$2 each in today's money.

1876

81

It is said that U.S. President Andrew Jackson's pet parrot squawked so many **CURSE WORDS** that he was removed from his master's **FUNERAL SERVICE.**

1837

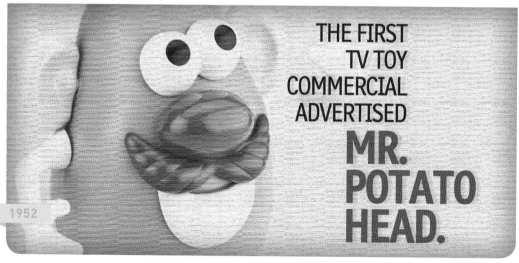

THE FIRST
TV TOY
COMMERCIAL
ADVERTISED
**MR.
POTATO
HEAD.**

1952

Ancient Persians began dyeing eggs for spring festivals about 5,000 years ago.

ca 3000 B.C.

Some **Vikings** bleached their hair and beards **blond**

A.D. 700–1100

Samurai warriors were paid with

RICE.

1603–1867

83

To smell sweet, ancient Egyptians wore melting lumps of perfumed wax on their heads.

Egypt no longer allows Tut's mask to travel outside the country.

King Tut's mask is made of 24 pounds (11 kg) of solid gold—that's the weight of a small dog!

Kids in ancient Egypt didn't wear any clothes.

84

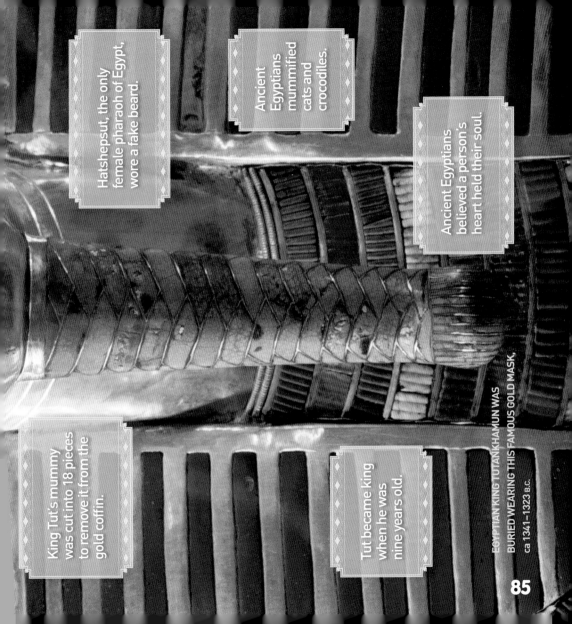

Hatshepsut, the only female pharaoh of Egypt, wore a fake beard.

Ancient Egyptians mummified cats and crocodiles.

Ancient Egyptians believed a person's heart held their soul.

King Tut's mummy was cut into 18 pieces to remove it from the gold coffin.

Tut became king when he was nine years old.

EGYPTIAN KING TUTANKHAMUN WAS BURIED WEARING THIS FAMOUS GOLD MASK, ca 1341–1323 B.C.

ANCIENT GREEKS BELIEVED THAT LETTUCE JUICE COULD **HELP YOU SLEEP.**

1930s

To reassure fearful passengers, the first airlines hired *only* REGISTERED NURSES to be stewardesses.

1927

The first giant helium balloon used in the Macy's Thanksgiving Day Parade in New York flew away and popped after the event.

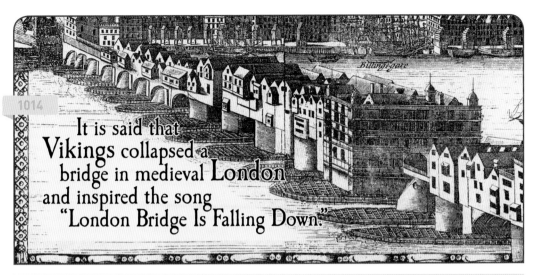

1014

It is said that Vikings collapsed a bridge in medieval London and inspired the song "London Bridge Is Falling Down."

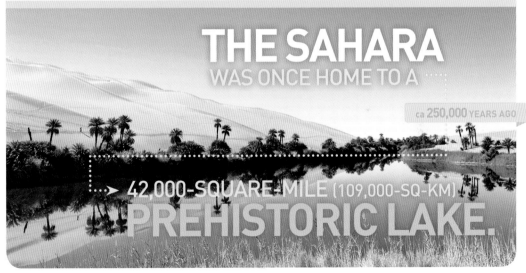

THE SAHARA
WAS ONCE HOME TO A

ca 250,000 YEARS AGO

42,000-SQUARE-MILE (109,000-SQ-KM) PREHISTORIC LAKE.

SNAIL

WERE USED AS A CURRENCY IN

SHELLS

CHA-CHING!

FORM OF ANCIENT CHINA.

1500 B.C.

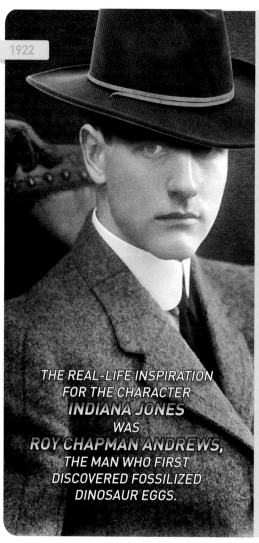

1922

THE REAL-LIFE INSPIRATION
FOR THE CHARACTER
INDIANA JONES
WAS
ROY CHAPMAN ANDREWS,
THE MAN WHO FIRST
DISCOVERED FOSSILIZED
DINOSAUR EGGS.

A worker digging a ditch in Bulgaria found a

☙

6,000-YEAR-OLD CEMETERY

☙

filled with gold artifacts.

1972

You could be
beheaded
for
drinking coffee
in 17th-century Turkey—
it was thought to cause
bad behavior.

One Christmas Eve
during **WORLD WAR I,** British
and German soldiers
stopped fighting and started
SINGING CAROLS together.

1914

DOUBLE DUTCH JUMP ROPE

IS NAMED AFTER DUTCH COLONISTS WHO INTRODUCED THE GAME TO NORTH AMERICA.

1600s

A.D. 589

The
Chinese
invented
toilet
paper.

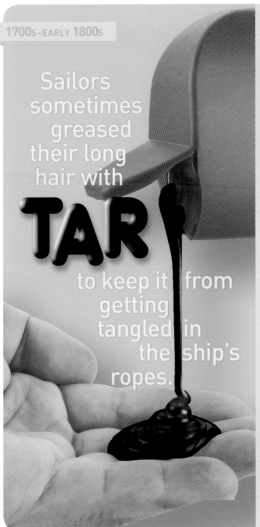

Sailors sometimes greased their long hair with

TAR

to keep it from getting tangled in the ship's ropes.

The first true **BASKETBALL** game was played with peach baskets, not hoops.

1891

For more than a thousand years, some people in Mongolia, Siberia, and China used **BRICKS OF TEA** as money.

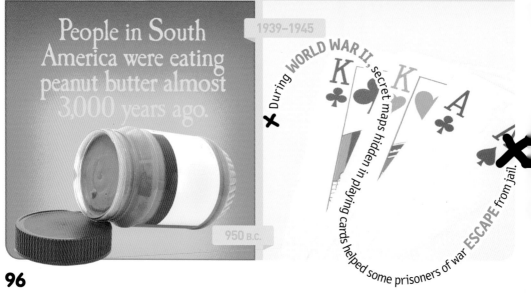

People in South America were eating peanut butter almost 3,000 years ago.

950 B.C.

1939–1945

During **WORLD WAR II**, secret maps hidden in playing cards helped some prisoners of war **ESCAPE** from jail.

THE INFAMOUS PIRATE

Blackbeard

TIED

smoking fuses

TO HIS BEARD TO SCARE OFF ENEMIES.

EARLY 1700s

1717

When

BEN FRANKLIN

was 11 years old, he invented

FINS

FOR HIS HANDS

to help him swim faster.

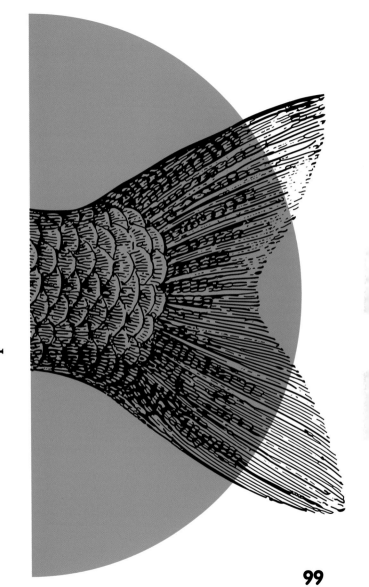

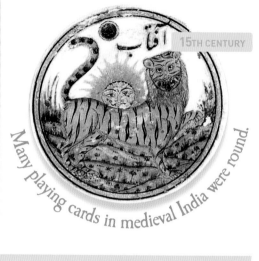

1920s

15TH CENTURY

Many playing cards in medieval India were round.

1600s

Flagpole sitting competitions

(seeing how long someone could sit on top of a flagpole) were once popular in the United States.

SPICES LIKE **CINNAMON** AND **CLOVES** WERE ONCE SO VALUABLE THAT WARS WERE FOUGHT OVER THEM.

An Englishman once **PEDDLED AROUND THE WORLD** on a big-wheeled bicycle called a penny-farthing.

1884–1886

Young Roman Emperor **Elagabalus** often seated his dinner guests on

"whoopee cushions."

A.D. 218–222

ANCIENT SCYTHIAN WARRIORS IN ASIA **POISONED THEIR ARROWS WITH SNAKE VENOM,** ANIMAL DROPPINGS, AND BLOOD.

1616

Playwright William Shakespeare's tombstone has a

CURSE

engraved on it to keep grave robbers away.

GOOD FREND FOR IESVS SAKE FORBEARE,
TO DIGG THE DVST ENCLOASED HEARE.
BLESE BE Ƴ MAN Ƴ SPARES THES STONES,
AND CVRST BE HE Ƴ MOVES MY BONES.

103

1854

THE LARGEST NUGGET FOUND DURING THE CALIFORNIA GOLD RUSH WEIGHED 195 POUNDS (88.5 KG)—AS MUCH AS A

large kangaroo!

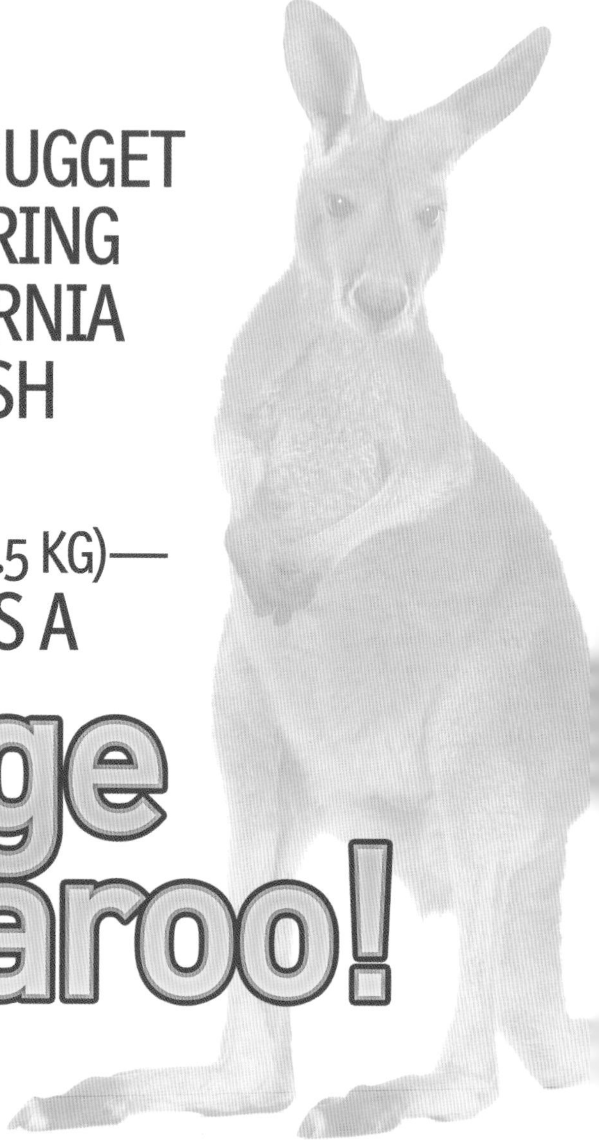

EARLY

GOLF
BALLS

WERE
FEATHER-FILLED
LEATHER POUCHES.

1940

Four teenagers discovered 17,000-year-old cave paintings by **FOLLOWING THEIR DOG INTO A HOLE** leading into France's Lascaux caves.

THE U.S. **POSTAL SERVICE** ONCE DELIVERED MAIL TO A U.S. MILITARY BASE INSIDE **GUIDED ROCKET MISSILES.**

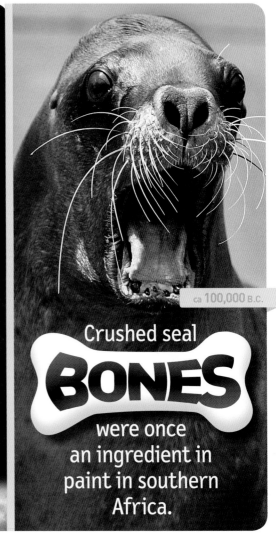

ca 100,000 B.C.

Crushed seal **BONES** were once an ingredient in paint in southern Africa.

108

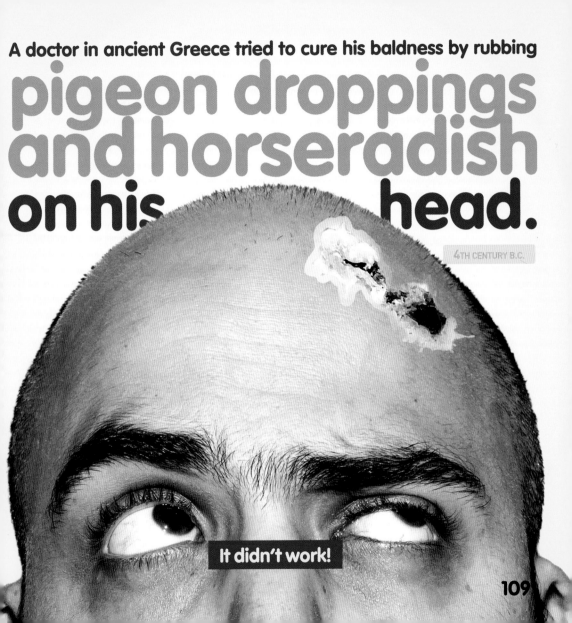

A doctor in ancient Greece tried to cure his baldness by rubbing **pigeon droppings and horseradish on his head.**

4TH CENTURY B.C.

It didn't work!

109

The word "rubber" comes from the erasers made of latex gum, which "rubbed" out pencil marks.

One of the oldest maps in the world was drawn on a mammoth tusk.

10,000 B.C.

It was **illegal** to **kiss your wife** in public in some parts of colonial **America.**

1600s

To scare away American Indians, a group of explorers sailed U.S. rivers in a steamboat that looked like a **FIRE-BREATHING SERPENT.**

1819

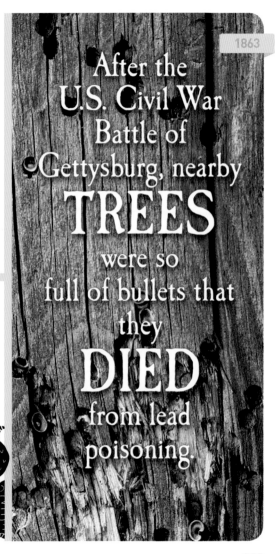

1863

After the U.S. Civil War Battle of Gettysburg, nearby **TREES** were so full of bullets that they **DIED** from lead poisoning.

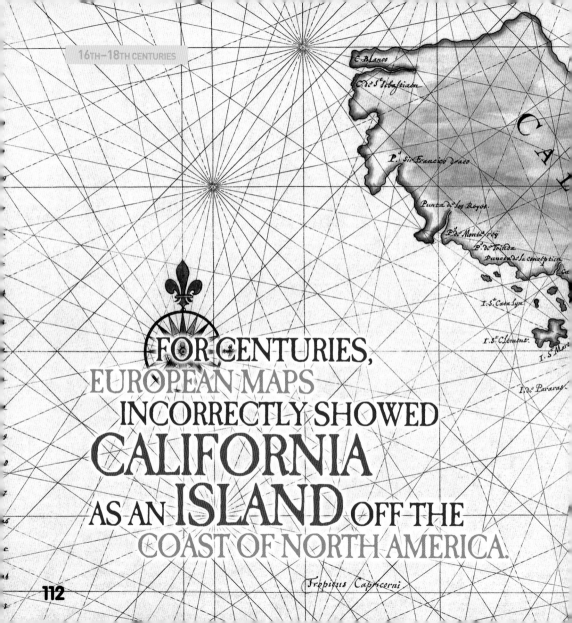

C. Blanco

C. de S.t Sebastiaon

CA

P.t. San Francisco draco

Punta de los Reyos

P.to de Monte rrey
P. de Trinida
Punta de la conceptice

I. S.t Cata lyn

I. S. Clemint
I. S. Mar

I. de Paraxes

FOR CENTURIES,
EUROPEAN MAPS
INCORRECTLY SHOWED
CALIFORNIA
AS AN ISLAND OFF THE
COAST OF NORTH AMERICA.

Tropicus Capricorni

112

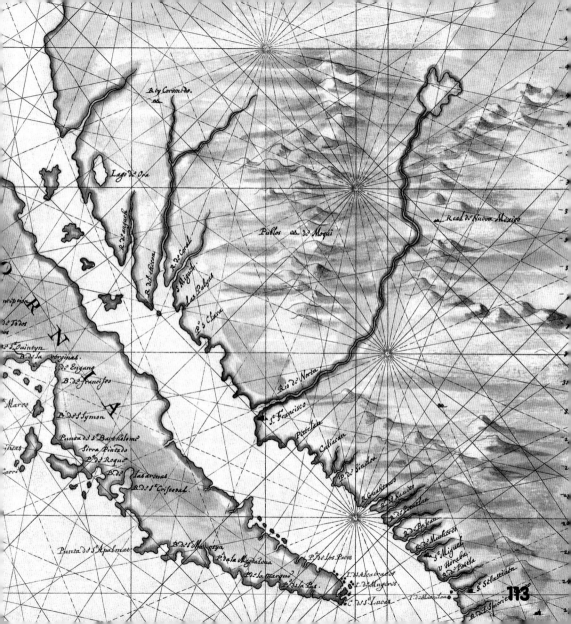

B. de Corōdo.

Lago de Ora

R. de Ayuck

Pablos de Moqui

Read de Nueva Mexico

R. de Stiteuni
R. de Corali
S. Miguel
Las Bolgas

P. s Clara

C

R

R. de las vorginas
de Engano
B. de Francisco

S. Quintyn

Rio de Nort

N

Y

B. de S. Symon

S. Francisco

Punta de S. Barthelomé
Sirra Pintado
B. de Roque
B. de las arēnas
B. de S. Crisoval

Marco

Pixicate

Culiacan

P. de Sinalos
R. Guabicaro
B. de Nabes
Pta. Lau
B. de Balean
B. de Machares
S. Miguel
v. Horaba
B. de Patela

Carri

S. Sebastian

Punta de S. Apalmat

B. de S. Martyn

P. de la Magdalena

P. de los Pecos

P. de la Margen
P. Isla Paz
C. de S. Lucas

T. de S. Alcabrado
T. de Mayares
T. de Mazalan

B. de Spirit.

113

Legend has it that England's Queen Elizabeth II's mom grew up in a

HAUNTED CASTLE.

1900s

525 B.C.

AN ARMY OF 50,000 PERSIAN SOLDIERS ONCE DISAPPEARED IN THE DESERTS OF EGYPT, NEVER TO BE SEEN AGAIN.

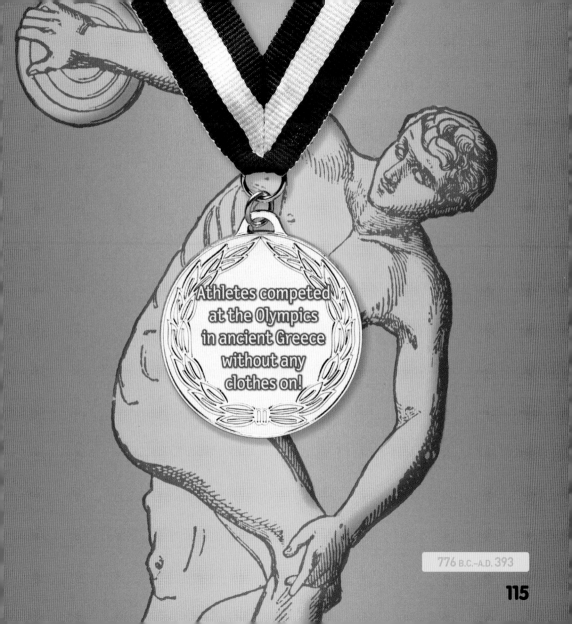

Athletes competed
at the Olympics
in ancient Greece
without any
clothes on!

776 B.C.–A.D. 393

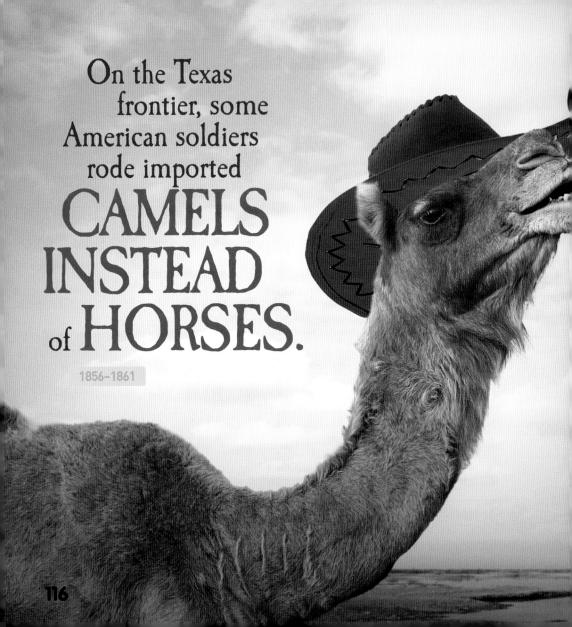

On the Texas frontier, some American soldiers rode imported

CAMELS
INSTEAD
of HORSES.

1856–1861

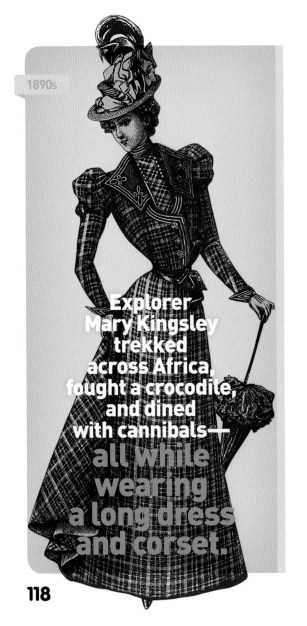

1890s

Explorer Mary Kingsley trekked across Africa, fought a crocodile, and dined with cannibals— all while wearing a long dress and corset.

Cats were considered sacred in ancient Egypt— the penalty for killing one was... DEATH!

3000–342 B.C.

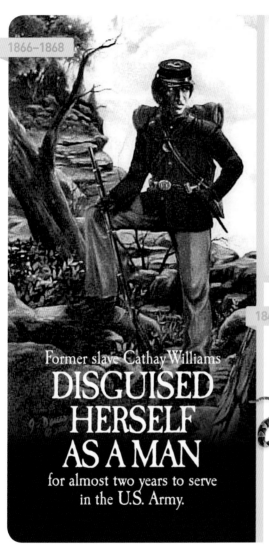

Former slave Cathay Williams
DISGUISED HERSELF AS A MAN
for almost two years to serve
in the U.S. Army.

QUEEN ELIZABETH I'S GODSON INVENTED THE FIRST FLUSHING TOILET.

ca 1591

184 B.C.

A ruthless general named
Hannibal bombed
enemy ships with pots full of
VENOMOUS SNAKES.

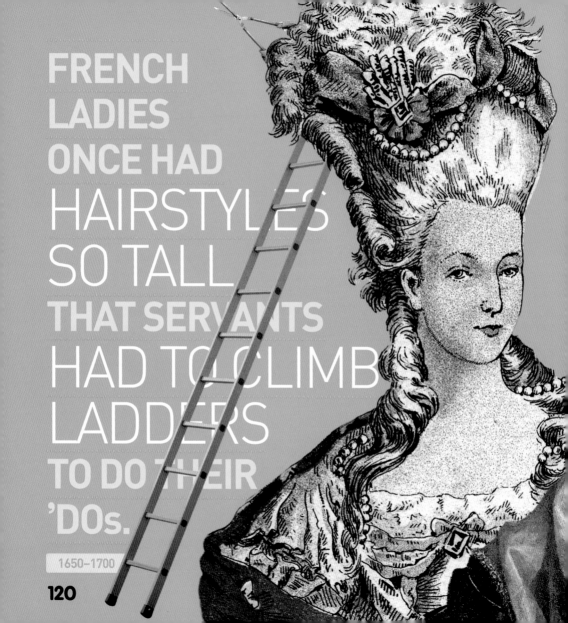

FRENCH LADIES ONCE HAD HAIRSTYLES SO TALL THAT SERVANTS HAD TO CLIMB LADDERS TO DO THEIR 'DOs.

1650–1700

120

X-ray Vision

BALD FRENCH KING **LOUIS XIII** MADE IT FASHIONABLE FOR 17TH-CENTURY MEN TO WEAR WIGS.

1610–1643

121

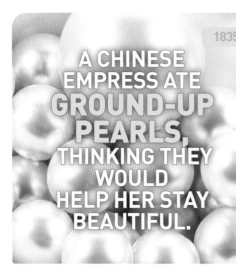

A CHINESE EMPRESS ATE **GROUND-UP PEARLS,** THINKING THEY WOULD HELP HER STAY BEAUTIFUL.

1835–1908

DIED 1809

AFTER FAMOUS COMPOSER FRANZ JOSEPH HAYDN DIED, GRAVE ROBBERS STOLE HIS BODY TO STUDY HIS HEAD.

In medieval Europe, soldiers sometimes flung **animal droppings** over castle walls during attacks.

13TH–15TH CENTURIES

Legend has it that the fierce conqueror Attila the Hun **DIED FROM A NOSEBLEED.**

A.D. 453

123

A.D. 500–1500

SOME MEDIEVAL CASTLE WALLS WERE AS THICK AS **THREE KING-SIZE BEDS.**

At weddings in ancient Rome, it was customary for the groom to **smash a barley cake over the** bride's head.

125

1842

A famous **NEW YORK CITY SHOWMAN** exhibited a mummified monkey torso with a sewn-on fish tail and claimed it was a real

MER

MAID.

The mummy of Russian revolutionary **Vladimir Lenin**, who **died in 1924**, is still on public display in Moscow, Russia.

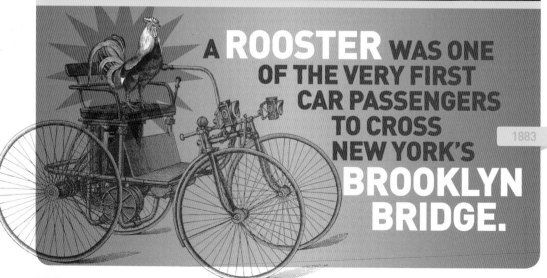

A **ROOSTER** WAS ONE OF THE VERY FIRST CAR PASSENGERS TO CROSS NEW YORK'S **BROOKLYN BRIDGE.**

1883

2010 **Workers uncovered the remains of an 18TH-CENTURY SHIP in a New York City construction site.**

1927

THE INVENTOR OF SLICED BREAD USED METAL PINS TO KEEP LOAVES TOGETHER BEFORE HE THOUGHT TO STICK THEM IN BAGS.

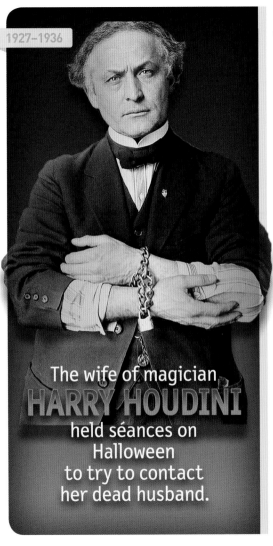

1927–1936

The wife of magician
HARRY HOUDINI
held séances on
Halloween
to try to contact
her dead husband.

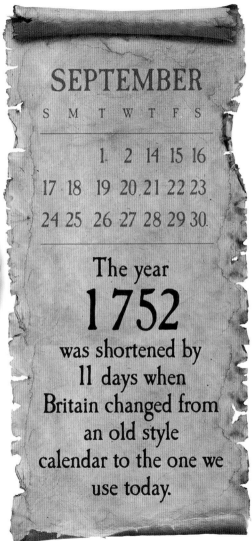

SEPTEMBER

S	M	T	W	T	F	S
		1	2	14	15	16
17	18	19	20	21	22	23
24	25	26	27	28	29	30

The year
1752
was shortened by
11 days when
Britain changed from
an old style
calendar to the one we
use today.

MOUNTAIN PEOPLE IN EUROPE BLEW

WOODEN

TO SIGNAL TO EACH OTHER ACROSS THE PEAKS.

HORNS

KING RAMA IV
OF SIAM (THAILAND)
OFFERED TO SEND
ELEPHANTS
TO THE UNITED STATES
AS A GIFT; PRESIDENT
ABRAHAM LINCOLN
**TURNED
HIM DOWN.**

A French officer who had lost his hand in battle got a mechanical replacement

OVER 460 YEARS AGO!

1550

1860

THE FIRST TRAFFIC LIGHT

WAS INTRODUCED IN LONDON, DECADES BEFORE MOTORIZED CARS WERE ON THE ROADS.

Russian ruler **TSAR PETER THE GREAT** was also an amateur dentist.

1682–1725

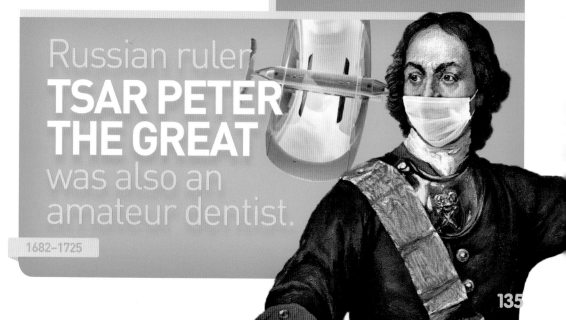

135

Wildcats started hanging out with humans when people started farming and storing grain, which led to lots of mice running around.
ca 8000 B.C.

In the 14th century, cats were outcasts because they were associated with witches.
1300s

Felix the cat was launched into space and retrieved (alive!) after descending to Earth in a special parachute designed by scientists.
1963

All house cats are descended from one kind of wildcat in the Middle East.

U.S. CIA spies placed listening devices on cats so the felines could pick up Soviet conversations from park benches and window sills.
1960s

King Charles I —who ruled Great Britain and Ireland— kept a black cat for good luck.
1640s

The first domestic cats in North America arrived on boats with the Pilgrims.
1600s

A wealthy Italian woman left $13 million to her cat, named Tommaso.
2011

137

THE DUTCH WERE OFFICIALLY IN A STATE OF WAR WITH

GREAT BRITAIN'S ISLES OF SCILLY

FOR 335 YEARS.

1651–1986

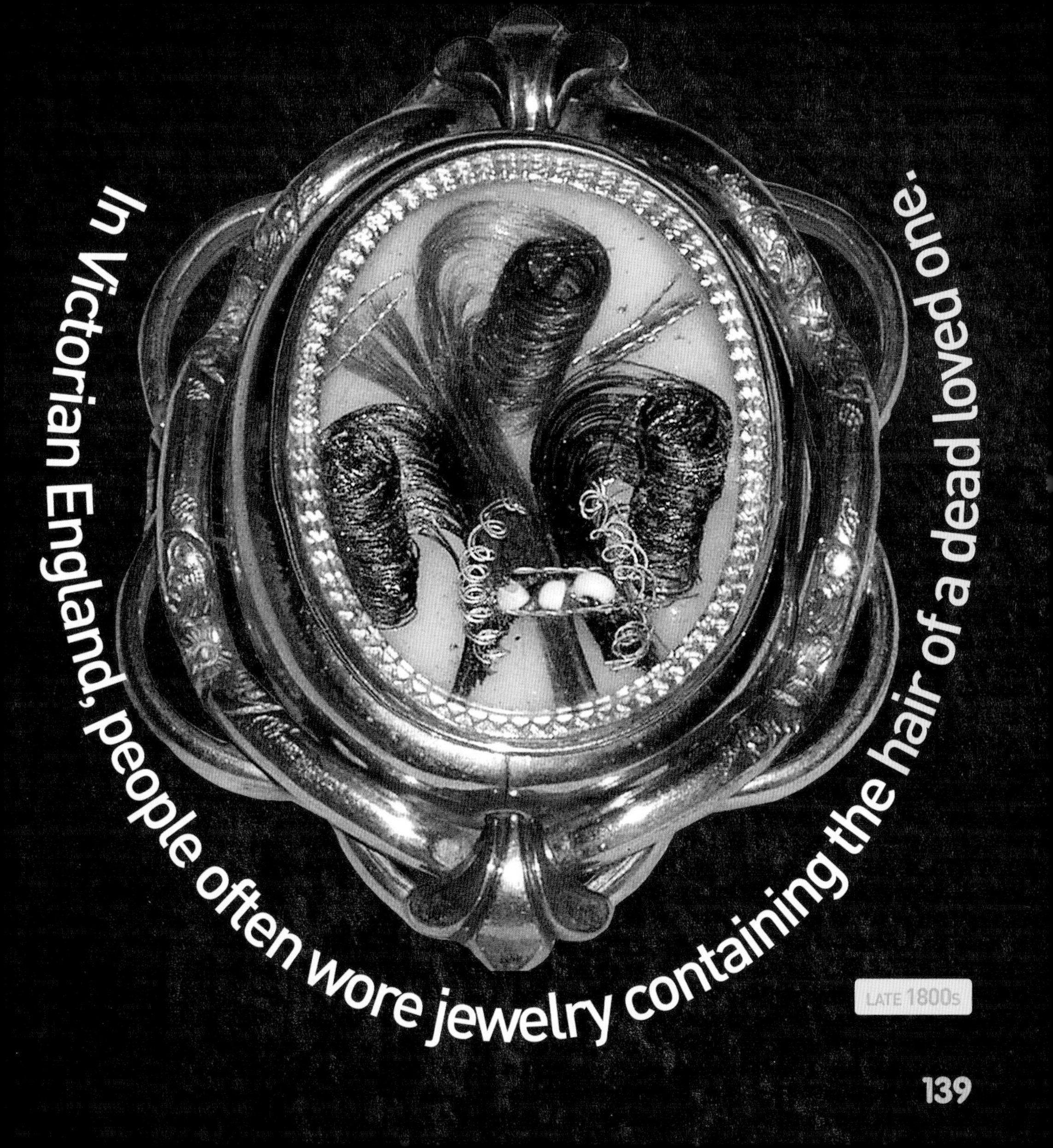

In Victorian England, people often wore jewelry containing the hair of a dead loved one.

LATE 1800s

139

21,000 B.C.

Early humans
used sharpened
**SNAIL
SHELLS**
as fishing hooks.

ΠΟΤΑΜΩΝΟΣ
ΤΩΛΕΣΒΟΝΑΚΤΟΣ
ΠΡΟΕΔΡΙΑ

15

700 B.C.–A.D. 600

Most ancient
Greek furniture
had three legs.

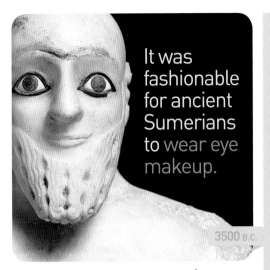

It was fashionable for ancient Sumerians to wear eye makeup.

3500 B.C.

800 B.C.–A.D. 476

Dormouse was considered a delicacy in ancient Rome.

2012

MODERN RUSSIAN SCIENTISTS GREW A FLOWER FROM

30,000-YEAR-OLD SEEDS

THAT HAD BEEN PRESERVED IN PERMAFROST.

THE "MONA LISA," painted in the 1500s, became famous only when art thieves **STOLE IT** from a museum 400 years later.

1911

The Mona Lisa
Leonardo daVinci

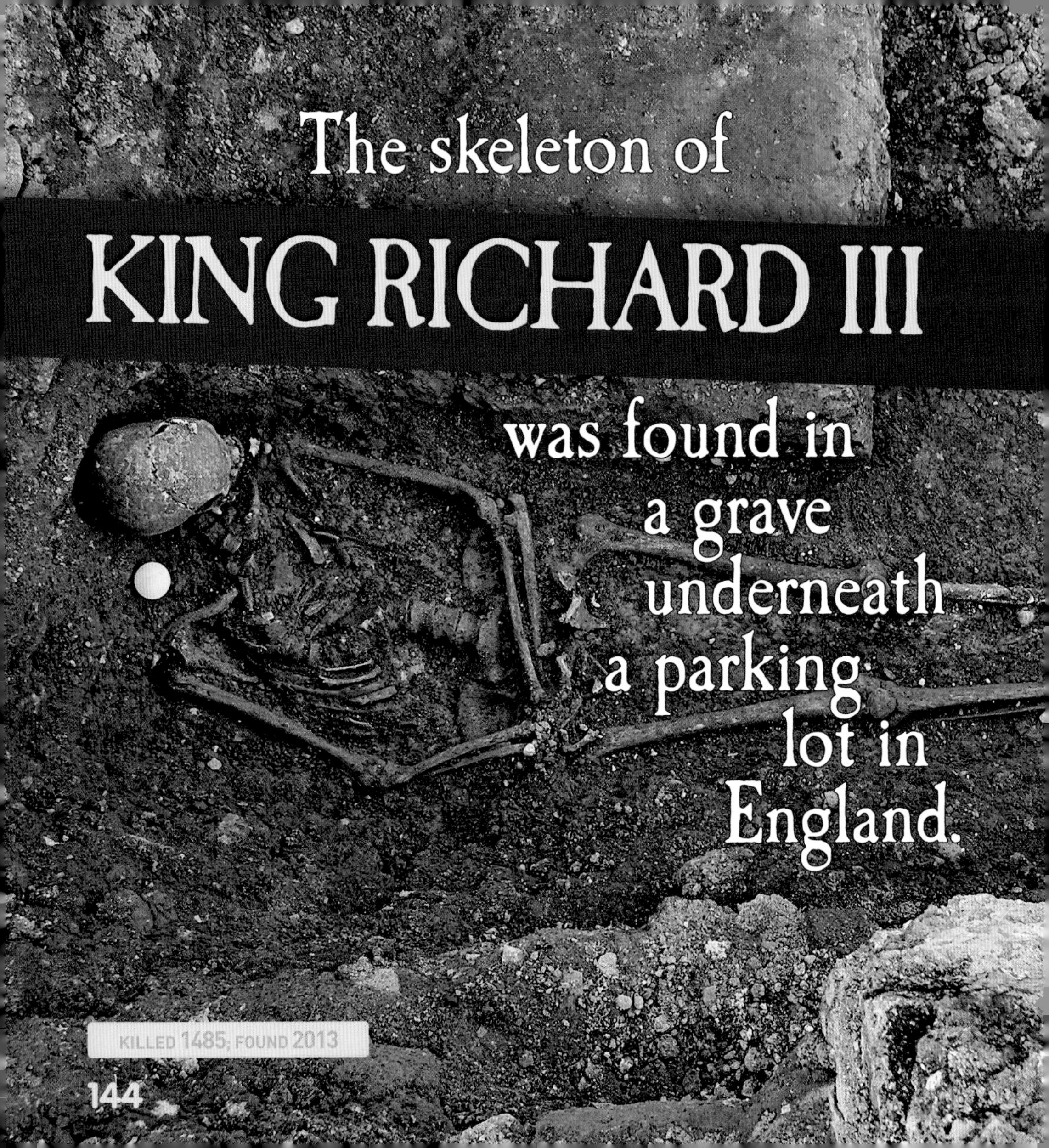

The skeleton of

KING RICHARD III

was found in
a grave
underneath
a parking
lot in
England.

KILLED 1485, FOUND 2013

144

Before **the Wright Brothers** achieved the first airplane flight, they **designed bicycles.**

1890s

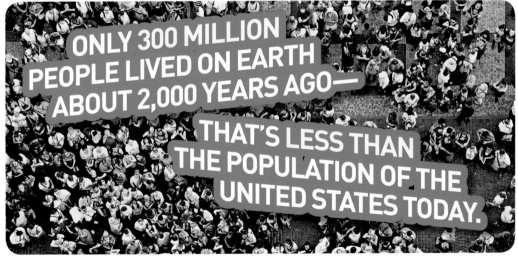

ONLY 300 MILLION PEOPLE LIVED ON EARTH ABOUT 2,000 YEARS AGO—

THAT'S LESS THAN THE POPULATION OF THE UNITED STATES TODAY.

German money was once so **worth** that a wheelbarrow full of the cash

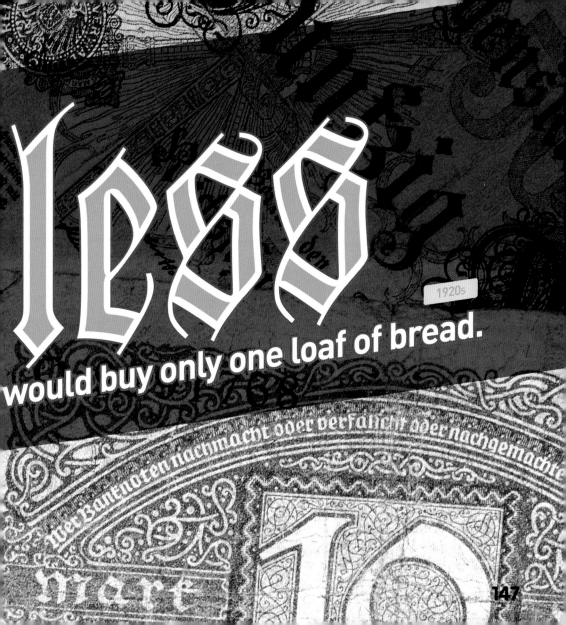

less

would buy only one loaf of bread.

1920s

A **5,500-YEAR-OLD LEATHER SHOE** WAS FOUND IN A MOUNTAIN CAVE IN ARMENIA.

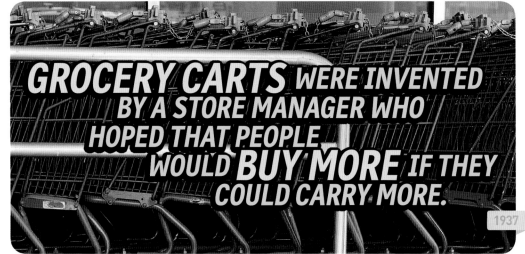

*GROCERY CARTS WERE INVENTED BY A STORE MANAGER WHO HOPED THAT PEOPLE WOULD **BUY MORE** IF THEY COULD CARRY MORE.*

Still popular today, **BULL LEAPING**— doing somersaults over the backs of angry bulls.— was a **POPULAR SPORT** on the island of Crete.

2000 B.C.

149

THE BIGGEST ROCKS AT
STONEHENGE
WEIGH
AS
MUCH
AS

BUILT 2500 B.C.

20 PICKUP TRUCKS.

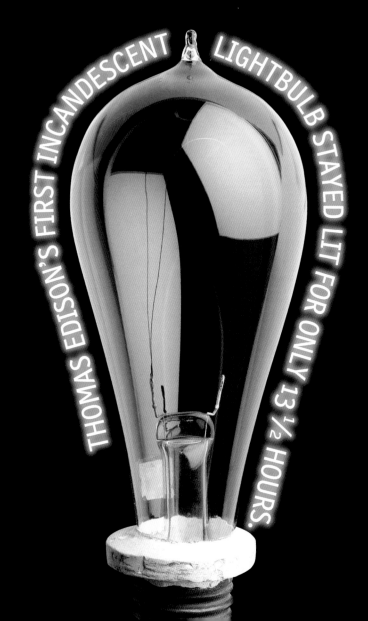

THOMAS EDISON'S FIRST INCANDESCENT LIGHTBULB STAYED LIT FOR ONLY 13 ½ HOURS.

1879

152

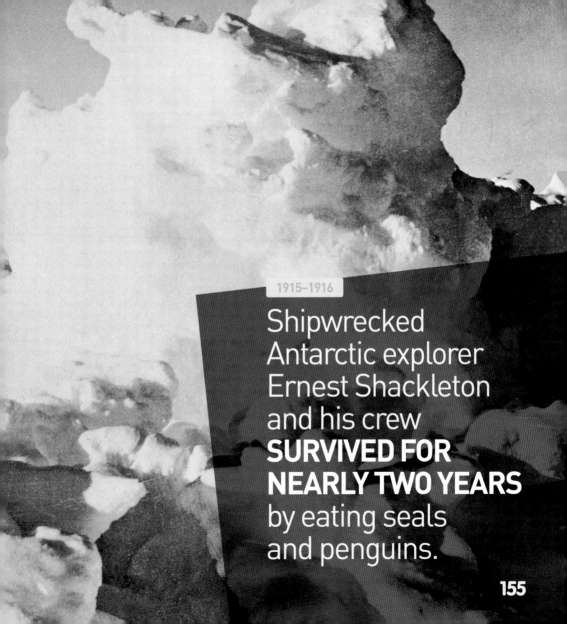

1915–1916

Shipwrecked Antarctic explorer Ernest Shackleton and his crew **SURVIVED FOR NEARLY TWO YEARS** by eating seals and penguins.

ARCHAEOLOGISTS DISCOVERED A 4,000-YEAR-OLD BOWL OF NOODLES IN CHINA.

DISCOVERED 2005

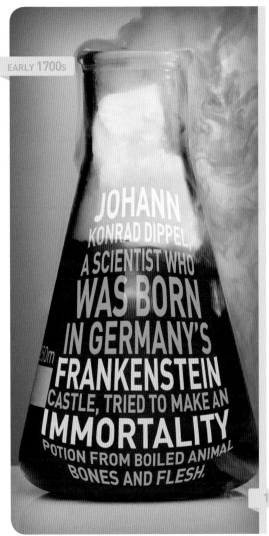

JOHANN KONRAD DIPPEL, A SCIENTIST WHO WAS BORN IN GERMANY'S FRANKENSTEIN CASTLE, TRIED TO MAKE AN IMMORTALITY POTION FROM BOILED ANIMAL BONES AND *FLESH.*

1896

The shortest war in history—between the United Kingdom and Zanzibar—lasted less than 45 minutes.

157

Some of the earliest **BICYCLES** had no **PEDALS**.

1817

THE WORLD'S FIRST WATERBEDS WERE MADE FROM WATER-FILLED GOATSKINS.

1600 B.C.

368 YEARS AFTER ARCHBISHOP THOMAS BECKET DIED, ENGLAND'S KING HENRY VIII ORDERED HIS BONES BE DUG UP, PUT ON TRIAL, AND BURNED.

1538

159

THE EIFFEL TOWER WAS MEANT TO BE A TEMPORARY EXHIBIT

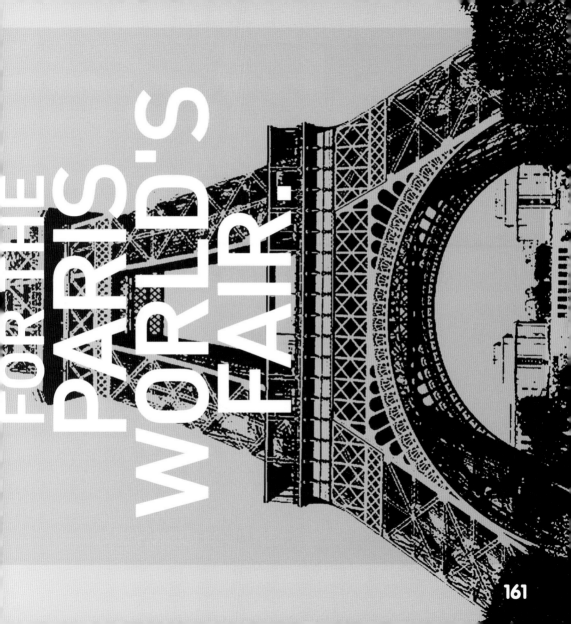

FOR THE PARIS WORLD'S FAIR.

Some fashionable Englishmen wore pointy shoes that stretched nearly two feet long

1300s

(.6 m)

1368–1644

Parts of
THE GREAT WALL OF CHINA
are held together by mortar
MADE FROM RICE.

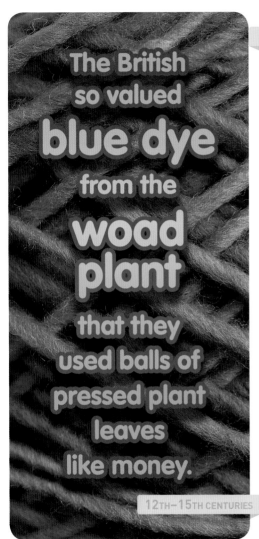

The British so valued **blue dye** from the **woad plant** that they used balls of pressed plant leaves like money.

1908

XUANTONG, THE VERY **LAST EMPEROR OF CHINA,** BECAME THE COUNTRY'S RULER WHEN HE WAS BARELY **THREE YEARS OLD.**

FAMOUS ARTIST
PABLO PICASSO'S FULL NAME

Pablo Diego José Nepomuceno María Cipriano de la Martyr Patricio Clito

IS 23 WORDS LONG.

Francisco de Paula Juan
de los Remedios
Santísima Trinidad
Ruíz y Picasso.

A RADIO PLAY ABOUT AN ALIEN INVASION WAS SO REALISTIC THAT THOUSANDS PANICKED, CERTAIN THAT MARTIANS WERE ACTUALLY ATTACKING EARTH.

1938

600 pigeons delivered the world's

FIRST AIRMAIL
from Lebanon to Egypt —

A.D. 975

each carried a

CHERRY
in a silk bag.

1643–1715

France's King
LOUIS XIV
had tiny
BATTLE SCENES
painted on the high
heels of his shoes.

800s–700s B.C.

Ancient Iraqis made life preservers out of inflated animal bladders.

22,000 people and
lived with the King of France

6,000 horses
in his palace at Versailles.

1661–1715

169

To cheer them up, World War I soldiers were given harmonicas.

Instead of flags, Mongol conqueror **GENGHIS KHAN** flew the **TAILS OF NINE WHITE YAKS.**

Yak hair!

13TH CENTURY

LONG BEFORE AIRPLANES WERE INVENTED, PERU'S NASCA INDIANS ETCHED ANIMAL SHAPES INTO THE LAND

THAT WERE SO HUGE YOU COULD SEE THE COMPLETE IMAGES ONLY FROM THE SKY.

200 B.C.

The game of **hopscotch** began as a **exercise** training for ancient

Roman

soldiers.

800 B.C.–A.D. 476

In imperial China,

ONLY THE IMPERIAL FAMILY

was allowed
to wear yellow.

LATE 14TH–EARLY 20TH CENTURIES

The **first candy canes had no stripes.** 1600s

1200s–1600s

EARLY CLOCKS had only one hand—or **NO HANDS** at all!

Some ancient people believed that **ventriloquists** had talkative spirits inside their stomachs.

ca 6TH CENTURY B.C.

CARNIVAL STUNTMAN FRANK "CANNONBALL" RICHA

SHOT IN THE BELL

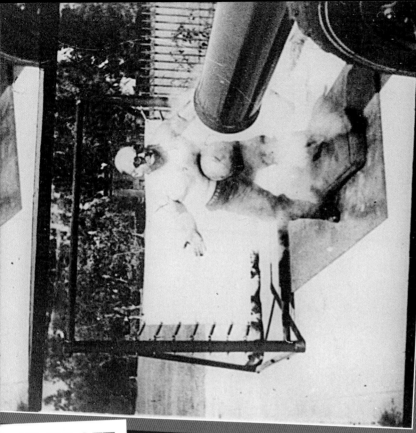

Don't try this
at home!

1930s

USED TO GET

WITH A CANNON . . .

TWICE A DAY.

QUEEN VICTORIA employed a royal RAT CATCHER.

1837–1901

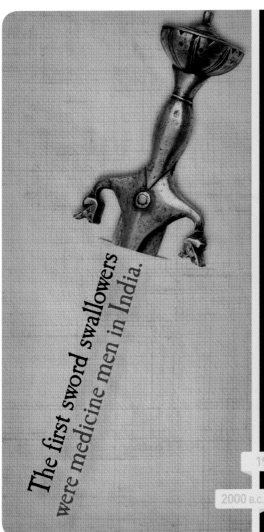

The first sword swallowers were medicine men in India.

The very **first image shown on TV** was of Stookie Bill, a ventriloquist's dummy.

1925

2000 B.C.

179

1600–1300 B.C.

Ancient Greek warriors studded their helmets with tusk slivers from **WILD PIGS.**

A scientist who helped design the first atomic bomb also created **THE FIRST VIDEO GAME.**

1958

1912

THREE DOGS WERE AMONG THOSE RESCUED FROM THE SINKING **TITANIC.**

Mexican revolutionary leader **PANCHO VILLA** worked with Hollywood moviemakers to film his battles during the **MEXICAN REVOLUTION.**

1914

About 8 million mummified dogs were buried in secret tunnels in an Egyptian desert—a dedication to Anubis, the jackal-headed god of the afterlife.
500 B.C.

Tiny lapdogs were a sign of wealth in medieval Europe.
A.D. 500–1500

Migaloo the black lab is trained to find artifacts and can sniff out 600-year-old bones in less than two minutes.

Wild dogs called dingoes were likely introduced to Australia by sailors from India.
2000 B.C.

A pooch named Stubby, a mascot for the U.S. Army during World War I, could salute with his paw.
1917–1918

Nine different male collies played Lassie, the female canine star of a classic TV show.
Show ran 1954–1971

A dogsled team traveled nearly 700 miles (1,100 km) in extreme weather to deliver lifesaving medical supplies to Nome, Alaska, U.S.A.
1925

The first animal to orbit Earth was Laika, a terrier mix who rode aboard the Soviets' Sputnik II spacecraft.
1957

Dogs have been "man's best friend" for at least 14,000 years.

The Chinese started building the Great Wall some **2,000 YEARS** before the Pilgrims arrived in America.

3RD CENTURY B.C.

once an Olympic sport.

Giant moai statues on Easter Island in the South Pacific each weigh as much as 500 gorillas.

1400–1600 A.D.

One of the earliest U.S. films showed

A MAN SNEEZING.

1894

THE FIRST 13 OLYMPICS HAD ONLY ONE EVENT: A SHORT RUNNING RACE.

SOUTH AMERICANS used to make cloth out of tree bark.

2000 B.C.

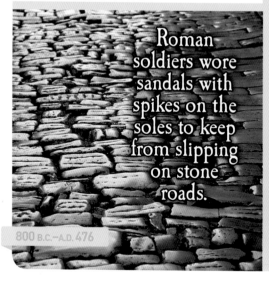

Roman soldiers wore sandals with spikes on the soles to keep from slipping on stone roads.

800 B.C.–A.D. 476

Queen Anne's Revenge—Blackbeard's famous pirate ship—weighed as much as **60 ELEPHANTS.**

1717–1718

PEOPLE HAVE TRAINED **FALCONS** TO HUNT FOR THEM FOR MORE THAN 4,000 YEARS.

In 1904, a man with a WOODEN LEG won three Olympic gold medals in GYMNASTICS.

THERE WAS AN OUTBREAK OF CONTAGIOUS LAUGHTE IN AN AFRICAN TOWN THAT LASTED FOR SIX MONTHS STRAIGHT!

IN THE
LATE 19TH
CENTURY,
AN AMERICAN
WOMAN'S
OUTFIT COULD
WEIGH AS
MUCH AS
40 POUNDS
(18 KG)—THAT'S
AS HEAVY AS

NINE
BRICKS!

1520

FRENCH KING FRANCIS I

ONCE WON A WRESTLING MATCH AGAINST

ENGLISH KING HENRY VIII.

ca 3000 B.C.

FIVE THOUSAND YEARS AGO, EUROPEANS MADE ICE SKATES OUT OF ANIMAL BONES.

1415

The corpse of
William the Conqueror

BURST

when monks tried
to stuff his body into
a too-small coffin.

A.D. 173–238

7

6

5

4

3

2

1

0

Roman Emperor

Gaius Julius Verus Maximinus

was said to be more than eight feet (2.4 m) tall!

Ancient Greeks carried coins in their mouths because they didn't have pockets.

700 B.C.–A.D. 600

3000–342 B.C.

It took **70 days** to make an Egyptian mummy.

192

"Mona Lisa" does not have eyebrows.

1503–1506

A.D. 79

ALMOST 2,000 YEARS AFTER A VOLCANIC ERUPTION BURIED POMPEII, ARCHAEOLOGISTS DISCOVERED LOAVES OF BREAD STILL SITTING IN THE CITY'S OVENS.

193

At seven years old, Earhart made a backyard roller coaster using a wooden crate and roller-skate wheels.

Earhart had her own fashion line, which included shirts made of parachute silk.

On her nonstop flight across the Atlantic in 1932, Amelia Earhart did not eat or drink anything except tomato juice.

Upon completing her solo flight across the Atlantic Ocean, Earhart made an unexpected landing in a cow field in Ireland.

Earhart's childhood dog's name was James Ferocious.

Earhart once took First Lady Eleanor Roosevelt on a nighttime flight around Washington, D.C., U.S.A.

Earhart once toasted Britain's King George V with a glass of buttermilk.

Amelia Earhart
Born 1897; disappeared 1937

195

VIKING SHIPS

sailed at 10 knots
(19 km) per hour—
about the speed
that you ride
a bike!

The Maya were making rubber objects some

3,000 YEARS

before the material was patented in the United States.

1600 B.C.

It took about **490 feet** (150 m) of linen to wrap a mummy.

A NEARLY **5,000**-
YEAR-OLD SKELETON
HAS THE OLDEST
ARTIFICIAL EYE EVER
DISCOVERED.

DISCOVERED 2006

The world's
oldest wad of
**CHEWING
GUM**
is 9,000
years old.

DISCOVERED 1993

The first
electric car
was made
in 1891.

198

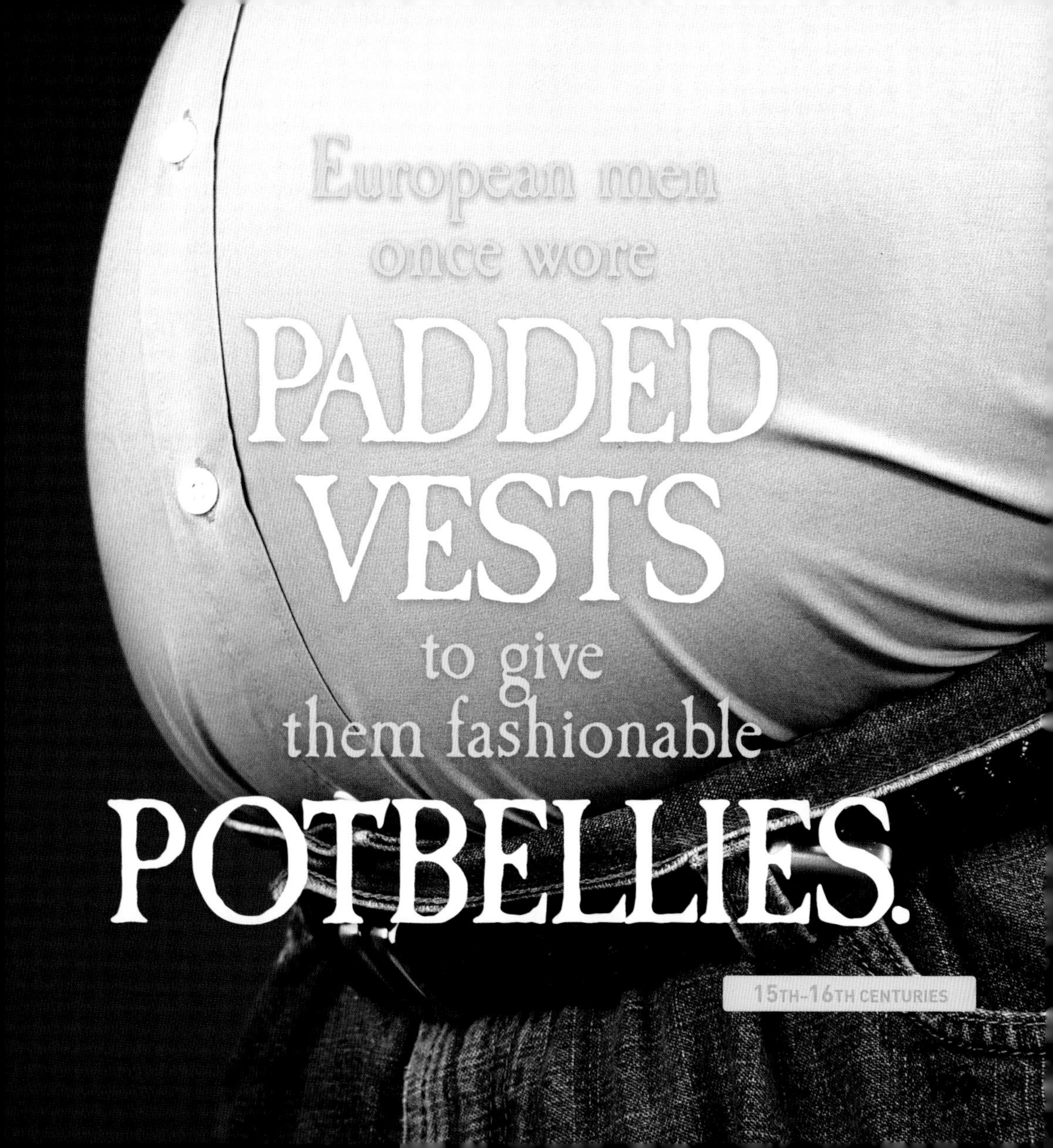

European men
once wore

PADDED
VESTS

to give
them fashionable

POTBELLIES.

15TH–16TH CENTURIES

Illustrations are indicated by **boldface.**

FACTFINDER

Since 1888, the National Geographic Society has funded more than 12,000 research, exploration, and preservation projects around the world. The Society receives funds from National Geographic Partners, LLC, funded in part by your purchase. A portion of the proceeds from this book supports this vital work. To learn more, visit natgeo.com/info.

For more information, please visit nationalgeographic.com, call 1-877-873-6846, or write to the following address:
National Geographic Partners
1145 17th Street N.W.
Washington, D.C. 20036-4688 U.S.A.

Prepared by the Book Division
Hector Sierra, *Senior Vice President and General Manager*
Nancy Laties Feresten, *Senior Vice President, Kids Publishing and Media*
Jennifer Emmett, *Vice President, Editorial Director, Children's Books*
Eva Absher-Schantz, *Design Director, Kids Publishing and Media*
Jay Sumner, *Director of Photography, Kids Publishing and Media*
R. Gary Colbert, *Production Director*
Jennifer A. Thornton, *Director of Managing Editorial*

Staff for This Book
Robin Terry, *Project Manager*
Amy Briggs, *Project Editor*
Eva Absher-Schantz, *Art Director*
Chad Tomlinson, *Designer*
Julie Beer, Michelle Harris, *Researchers*
Hillary Moloney, *Associate Photo Editor*
Callie Broaddus, *Design Production Assistant*
Ariane Szu-Tu, *Editorial Assistant*
Grace Hill, *Associate Managing Editor*
Joan Gossett, *Production Editor*
Lewis R. Bassford, *Production Manager*
Susan Borke, *Legal and Business Affairs*

Based on the "Weird But True" department in *National Geographic Kids* magazine

Production Services
Phillip L. Schlosser, *Senior Vice President*
Chris Brown, *Vice President, NG Book Manufacturing*
Nicole Elliott, *Manager*
Neal Edwards, *Imaging*

THAT'S WEIRD!

206

PHOTO CREDITS

Abbreviations: CB = Corbis; GI = Getty Images; IS = iStockphoto; NGS = National Geographic Stock; SS = Shutterstock; WMC = Wikimedia Commons

COVER and SPINE: wooden sign, frescomovie/SS; arrows, Sebastian Kaulitzki/SS; knight, Oleg Zhevelev/SS; 2 (Left), Oleg Zhevelev/SS; 3 (Top), frescomovie/SS; 3 (Top Center), Sebastian Kaulitzki/SS; 5, Yellowj/SS; 6 (Left), Richard Bergmann/GI; 6 (Top Right), adoc-photos/CB; 6 (Right Center), Rudmer Zwerver/IS; 6 (Bottom Right), Diane Labombarbe/IS; 6 (Bottom Left) r.martens/SS; 7, Bettmann/CB; 8 (Left, Right), Andrey_Kuzmin/SS; 8 (Center), andersphoto/SS; 9 (Top Left), Mediagram/SS; 9 (Top Center), Alexander A. Kataytsev/SS; 9 (Top Right), Karina Bakalyan/SS; 9 (Right Center), Larisa Bozhikova/IS; 9 (Bottom Left), heinteh5/SS; 9 (Bottom Right), GrigoryL/SS; 10–11, Predrag Vuckovic/IS; 12 (Top Left), Mark Evans/IS; 12 (Top Right), Lalan/SS; 12 (Bottom), Skalapendra/SS; 13 (Top Left), oneo/SS; 13 (Top Right), WMC; 13 (Bottom), Lia Koltyrina/SS; 14–15 (Bottom Left), jaroslava V/SS; 15 (Bottom Right), D. Hurst/Alamy; 16, Chris Hill/NGS; 17 (Inset), NTPL/John Hammond; 17 (Top Left), Victoria Chukalin/IS; 17 (Left), panbazil/SS; 17 (Bottom Right), Don Bayley/IS; 18, IlexImage/IS; 18 (Background), troyka/SS; 19 (Top Right), StudioSmart/SS; 20–21, holbox/SS; 22, Radius Images/Alamy; 23 (Top Right), WMC; 23 (Left), Vitaly Titov & Maria Sidelnikova/SS; 23 (Center), stevemart/SS; 23 (Inset), WilliamSherman/IS; 23 (Bottom Left), Vlad Trotsenko/SS; 24 (Top), tele52/SS; 24 (Bottom), Scott Rothstein/SS; 25 (Center), Africa Studio/SS; 25 (Background), Aliaksandr Mazurkevich/Alamy; 26–27, mashe/SS; 28 (Top), Marian Pentek/IS; 28 (Bottom), Tatiana Popova/SS; 29 (Top Left), Daniel R. Burch/IS; 29 (Top Right), prapass/SS; 29 (Left), Paolo Gaetano Rocco/IS; 29 (Bottom), Picsfive/SS; 30–31, Timothy Craig Lubcke/SS; 32, Sibrikov Valery/SS; 34, Lauri Patterson/IS; 35 (Top Left), udra/SS; 35 (Bottom), Bettmann/CB; 36, Photo Researchers RM/GI; 37, Nick Free/IS; 38 (Top), WimL/SS; 38 (Center), Maks Narodenko/IS; 38 (Bottom), AP Photo/Daniel Maurer; 38, Steven Wynn/IS; 39 (Top), Willie B.Thomas/IS; 39 (Left), WMC, National Portrait Gallery, London/Lady Jane Dudley by Unknown artist; 39 (Bottom), Stocksnapper/SS; 40–41, Jeannette Meier Kamer/IS; 42 (Top Left), Floortje/IS; 42 (Top Right), Kamira/SS; 42 (Bottom), Valentina_s/SS; 43 (Top Left), Library of Congress; 43 (Top Right), Iwona Grodzka/SS; 43 (Up Back), Elenamiv/SS; 43 (Bottom Left), Aksenova Natalya/SS; 43 (Bottom Right), panbazil/SS; 44 (Top), Sebastian Knight/SS; 44 (Bottom Left), Library of Congress; 45, Eric Isselée/SS; 45 (Center), Andrey Eremin/SS; 46, wiedzma/SS; 47, Lasse Kristensen/SS; 48 (Top Left), Manuela Weschke/IS; 48 (Top Center), Madlen/SS; 48 (Right), Laborant/SS; 48 (Bottom Left), Antagain/IS; 48 (Bottom Center), clu/IS; 49 (Left), Neveshkin Nikolay/SS; 49 (Right), Lukas Hlavac/SS; 50 (Top Left), Julian Rovagnati/SS; 50 (Right), Mark Blinch/Reuters/CB; 50 (Left Center), eAlisa/SS; 50 (Bottom Left), svand/SS; 51 (Left), Franck Boston/SS; 51 (Right), WMC; 52–53, NASA; 54 (Top), © USA Patents Office; 54 (Center), Marek Szumlas/SS; 54 (Bottom), Ian Nolan/Alamy; 55 (Top Background), bellenixe/SS; 55 (Top), Daniel Kerek/Alamy; 55 (Top Left), WMC; 55 (Top Right), Berents/SS; 55 (Bottom Left), Mishella/SS; 56, AP Photo/Thanassis Stavrakis; 57, Scott Hailstone/IS; 57 (Top Background), Daniel R Burch/IS; 57 (Center), Steve Collender/SS; 59 (Top), nito/SS; 60 (Top Left), Ivan Ponomarev/SS; 60 (Top Right), Matej Michelizza/IS; 60 (Center), Andriano/SS; 60 (Bottom Left), pixhook/IS; 60 (Bottom Right), Yuri Arcurs/SS; 61 (Left), Micha Rosenwirth/SS; 61 (Right), SuperStock RM/GI; 62, Photographer/SS; 64 (Left), Saime Deniz Tuyel Dogan/IS; 64 (Center), Mike Elliott/SS; 64 (Right), Reconstruction by Kennis © South Tyrol; 64 (Right Background), iofoto/SS; 65 (Top Left), fabio boari/IS; 65 (Top), Alan Uster/SS; 65 (Bottom Left), Robert Kyllo/IS; 68 (Top Left), Edward Fielding/SS; 68 (Bottom Left), eurobanks/SS; 68 (Right), Rob Hainer/SS; 68 (Back Right) Bellenixe/SS; 69 (Top Left), Daria Teplova/SS; 69 (Top Right), Dorling Kindersley/GI; 69 (Bottom), The British Library Board/GI; 70 (Left), © USA Patents Office; 70 (Right), Hulton Archive/GI; 71 (Top), Louis K. Meisel Gallery, Inc./CB; 71 (Bottom Left), Colleen Morgan; 71 (Bottom Right), Sonia Goncalves/SS; 72, Jamie Wilson/IS; 74 (Top), Photononstop RM/GI; 74 (Left), Ilya Akinshin/SS; 74 (Right), Prill/SS; 74, Annie Greenwood/SS; 75, Donald Gargano/SS; 75 (Inset), windu/SS; 76 (Background), Eric Isselée/IS; 76 (Center), Diane Diederich/IS; 76 (Bottom), tomgigabite/SS; 77 (Left Center), Nicku/SS; 77 (Right), Nicolas McComber/IS; 78, Sabri Deniz Kizil/SS; 80 (Top), Terry North/IS; 80 (Left), Eric Isselée/IS; 80 (Right Background), Winston Link/SS; 80 (Bottom), Vladimir Mucibabic/IS; 81 (Top), Nickola_Che/SS; 81 (Bottom Left), Denys Prokofyev/IS; 81 (Bottom Right), DNY59/IS; 82 (Top Left), Ronald Sumners/SS; 82 (Top Right), Eric Isselée/IS; 82 (Bottom), Catherine Lane/IS; 83 (Left), stishok/SS; 83 (Left Center), Robert Neumann/SS; 83 (Top Right), Bob Carey/GI; 83 (Bottom Right), ma-k/IS; 84, Kenneth Garrett/NGS; 86, Nils Z/SS; 86 (Bottom), Hulton Archive/GI; 87 (Top), WMC; 87 (Bottom), Patrick Poendl/SS; 88, Tarek El Sombati/IS; 90 (Top), David Morgan/IS; 90 (Right), SashaFoxWalters/IS; 90 (Bottom), WMC; 91 (Top), Kraska/SS; 91 (Bottom), Viktor Gladkov/SS; 92, DreamPictures/GI; 94, Dave White/SS; 95 (Top), Aaron Amat/SS; 95 (Left), sevenke/SS; 95 (Bottom), Sandy Sandy/IS; 96 (Top), Kadir Barcin/IS; 96 (Bottom Left), Jaimie Duplass/SS; 96 (Bottom Right), Jason Stitt/SS; 97, WMC; 98, Hein Nouwens/SS; 100 (Left), AP Photo; 100 (Top Right), Angelo Hornak/CB; 100 (Bottom Left), Giuliano Coman/SS; 101, Baris Simsek/IS; 102 (Left), Djomas/SS; 102 (Bottom), Oliver Leedham/Alamy; 102 (Background), ciarada/SS; 103 (Top Left), Malcolm Romain/IS; 103 (Top Right), Pete Oxford/Minden Pictures/GI;103 (Background), Ensuper/SS; 103 (Bottom), PoodlesRock/CB; 104, Eric Isselée/SS; 105, lzf/SS; 106, Hemis.fr RM/GI; 108 (Right), Reinhold Leitner/SS; 108 (Center), jimeone/SS; 108 (Bottom Center), Elena Moiseeva/SS; 108 (Bottom), conrado/SS; 109, Eugenio Marongiu/SS; 110 (Top), James Driscoll/IS; 110 (Bottom), Hein Nouwens/SS; 111 (Top Left), Lise Gagne/IS; 111 (Right), Dmitry Naumov/SS; 111 (Bottom Left), Complot/SS; 112, WMC; 114 (Bottom Left), Trevor Hunt/IS; 114 (Bottom Right), Pichugin Dmitry/SS; 115 (Background), Steven Wynn/IS; 115 (Center), Local Admin/IS; 116–117, Blend Images/John Lund/Stephanie Roeser/GI; 116 (Top), simpleman/SS; 117 (Top Center), andzhey/SS; 117 (Top Right), Basov Mikhail/SS; 118 (Left), AKaiser/SS; 118 (Right), Tatjana Romanova/IS; 119 (Left), John Will Davis/Encore Graphics & Fine Art; 119 (Top Right), Elnur/SS; 119 (Bottom Center), Eric Isselée/SS; 119 (Bottom Right), Sibrikov Valery/SS; 120 (Top Left), NinaMalyna/SS; 120 (Left), viphotos/SS; 120 (Right), Stefano Bianchetti/CB; 121 (Top), maga/SS; 121 (Bottom), Justus van Egmont/The Bridgeman Art Library/GI; 122 (Top Left), ANCH/SS; 122 (Top Right), aslysun/SS; 122 (Right), DEA/A. Dagli Orti/GI; 122 (Bottom Left), oblong1/SS; 123 (Left), PoodlesRock/CB; 123 (Center), yiapsf/IS; 124, Borja Andreu/SS; 125, Hein Nouwens/SS; 126, Vladyslav Danilin/SS; 127, Eric Isselée/IS; 128 (Top), Reuters/CB; 128 (Left Center), lynea/SS; 128 (Bottom Left), Hein Nouwens/SS; 129, SoRad/SS; 130, nito/SS; 131 (Left), Bettmann/CB; 131 (Right), Tischenko Irina/SS; 132–133, Per Breiehagen/GI; 134 (Left), Bettmann/CB; 134 (Center), topseller/SS; 134 (Right), jeep2499/SS; 135 (Top Right), omer sukru goksu/IS; 135 (Top Left), Tyler Olson/SS; 135 (Right Center), Hasloo Group Production Studio/SS; 135 (Bottom Right), WMC; 136, Vladyslav Starozhylov/SS; 137, loops7/IS; 138, Robert Harding World Imagery/GI; 139, Time Dances By; 139 (Background), magicoven/SS; 140 (Left), Institut für Ethnologie der Universität Göttingen; 140 (Right), Illustration for Trachten by Friedrich Hottenroth/The Bridgeman Art Library; 141 (Top Left), The Bridgeman Art Library/GI; 141 (Right), AP Photo/HO, the Institute of Cell Biophysics of the Russian Academy of Sciences; 141 (Bottom Left), Eric Isselée/SS; 143–143, The Power of Forever Photography/GI; 144, University of Leicester/CB; 145 (Top), Library of Congress – digital ve/Science Faction/CB; 145 (Bottom), Flickr RM/GI; 146–147, Taigi/SS; 148 (Top), AP Photo/Department of Archaeology University College Cork; 148 (Bottom), WMC; 149, AP Photo/Manu Fernandez; 150, Jitloac/SS; 151 (Top), L Barnwell/SS; 151 (Top Center), Margo Harrison/SS; 151 (Bottom), Risteski Goce/SS; 151 (Bottom Center), L Barnwell/SS; 151 (Top), L Barnwell/SS; 152, High Impact Photography/IS; 153 (Top), KKulikov/SS; 153 (Bottom), Sukhonosova Anastasia/SS; 154–155, Bettmann/CB; 156, Mingchai/Dreamstime; 157 (Left), Serrnovik/Dreamstime; 157 (Right), Alex Kalmbach/IS; 157 (Bottom), Sascha Burkard/SS; 158 (Top), WMC; 158 (Bottom), Anita Stizzoli/IS; 159, Frances Twitty/GI; 159 (Top), Tim McClean Photography/IS; 160–161, Dennis_dol... /Dreamstime; 162 (Top), David Gordon/SS; 162 (Top Back), Aleksandar Mijatovic/SS; 162 (Bottom), Somchai Som/SS; 163 (Left), Bob Turitz/IS; 163 (Right), WMC; 166, sad444/SS; 167 (Top Left), justdd/SS; 167 (Top Right), photomaru/IS; 167 (Bottom), Claudio Divizia/SS; 168–169, Kiev.Victor/SS; 170 (Top), Latviz/Dreamstime; 170 (Bottom), Pete Niesen/SS; 171, tr3gin/SS; 172 (Left), Spanic/IS; 172–173, Haslam Photography/SS; 173 (Bottom), Spanic/IS; 175 (Top), photastic/SS; 175 (Bottom Left), Michael McCloskey/IS; 175 (Bottom Right), Valerie Loiseleux/IS; 176, Imagno/Austrian Archives/GI; 178 (Left), terekhov igor/SS; 178 (Right), Anna Hoychuk/SS; 179 (Left Background), Andy Gehrig/IS; 179 (Left), Olemac/SS; 179 (Right), SSPL/Science Museum/GI; 180 (Left), WMC; 180 (Right), fckncg/SS; 181, WMC; 182–183, Eric Isselée/SS; 184–185 (Top), Picsfive/SS; 184 (Bottom), Jarno Gonzalez Zarraonandia/SS; 185 (Bottom Left), James P. Blair/NGS; 185 (Bottom Right), doglikehorse/SS; 186 (Left), Philip Lange/SS; 186 (Bottom Right), Johan Swanepoel/IS; 187, Fernando Cortes/SS; 188–189 (Background), Eky Studio/SS; 189 (Left), Anders Blomqvist/Lonely Planet Images/GI; 189 (Right), Tom Cockrem/Lonely Planet Images/GI; 190, Library of Congress; 190 (Right), DNY59/IS; 191 (Right), Rumo/SS; 192 (Top), Georgios Kollidas/SS; 192 (Bottom), The Print Collector/Alamy; 193 (Top), Andrew Howe/IS; 193 (Bottom), Scisetti Alfio/SS; 194–195, Bettmann/CB; 196 (Top Left), Danny Smythe/SS; 196 (Right), Julian Rovagnati/IS; 197, Federico Rostagno/SS; 198 (Top), Lonely/SS; 198 (Bottom), Horiyan/SS; 199, Suzanne Tucker/SS; 206, Oleg Zhevelev/SS

KNIGHTS, LORDS, LADIES, AND MORE!

Explore the amazing MIDDLE AGES!

Create your own madcap MEDIEVAL adventure!